Frederick William Faber

Oratory hymns

Frederick William Faber

Oratory hymns

ISBN/EAN: 9783741190049

Manufactured in Europe, USA, Canada, Australia, Japa

Cover: Foto ©Angelika Wolter / pixelio.de

Manufactured and distributed by brebook publishing software (www.brebook.com)

Frederick William Faber

Oratory hymns

CONTENTS.

	No. of Hymn.	Nos. of Tunes.
The Most Holy Trinity	1	1
The Eternal Father	2	3
Jesus, my God and my All	3	23
Jesus is God	4	66
The Eternal Spirit	5	3
Veni Creator	6	24
Veni Sancte Spiritus	7	43
Holy Ghost, come down upon Thy Children	8	57
The Infant Jesus	9	15
The Agony	10	16
Jesus crucified	11	3, 8
The Descent of Jesus to Limbus	12	38
Jesus risen	13	27
The Ascension	14	49, 62, 63
The Descent of the Holy Ghost	15	2, 62, 63
Corpus Christi	16	17
The Sacred Heart	17	37
The Precious Blood	18	4
Communion	19	30
Thanksgiving after Communion	20	58
The Immaculate Conception	21	11, 77
Sine Labe Originali Concepta	22	—
Immaculate! Immaculate!	23	38
Our Lady's Presentation	24	64
Our Lady's Expectation	25	7
The Purification	26	20
The Dolours of Our Lady	27	12
The Assumption	28	29
To our Blessed Lady	29	10
The Month of May	30	48, 76
Another Month of Mary	31	21
The Orphan's Consecration to Mary	32	6, 7
Sweet Mother-Maid	33	61
For the Souls in Purgatory	34	8
Hymn of St. Casimir	35	G
The Patronage of St. Joseph	36	26
Hymn to St. Joseph	37	9
St. Michael	38	65
St. Gabriel	39	46
The Guardian Angel	40	39
St. Peter and St. Paul	41	78
St. John the Evangelist	42	35
To our Holy Father, St. Philip Neri	43	62, 63
St. Philip's Penitents	44	5

CONTENTS.

	No. of Hymn.	Nos. of Tunes.
St. Philip's Picture	45	28, 62, 63
St. Philip's Charity	46	18
St. Philip's Death	47	43
St. Martin and St. Philip	48	65
St. Vincent of Paul	49	3'
St. Patrick's Day	50	50
St. Wilfrid	51	35
My Father	52	37
School Hymn	53	32
The True Shepherd	54	13, 79
Faith of our Fathers	55	14
Faith of our Fathers (for Ireland)	56	14
The Right must Win	57	62
The Eternal Years	58	64
The Sinner invited to the Mission	59	29
The Act of Contrition	60	22
Forgiveness of Injuries	61	36
The Wages of Sin	62	34
Distractions in Prayer	63	63
The Work of Grace	64	59
A Good Confession	65	19
The Remembrance of Mercy	66	42
The Pilgrims of the Night	67	54
The Christian's Song on his March to Heaven	68	55
Fight for Sion	69	67
Evening Hymn at the Oratory	70	25
The Memory of the Dead	71	41
Heaven	72	56
Paradise	73	40

PART II.

The Three Kings	74	—
St. Philip and the World	75	44
The Emigrant's Song	76	60

PART III.

Veni Creator	77	24
Te Deum laudamus	78	72
O salutaris Hostia	79	51, 71
Tantum ergo Sacramentum	80	52, 70
Adeste fideles	81	47
Magnificat	82	—
Litany of Loretto	83	53
Salve Regina	84	--
Ave maris stella	85	73
Way of the Cross	86	68
Stabat Mater	87	69
Miserere	88	75
De profundis	89	74
Lent	90	—

INDEX.

	No. of Hymn.	Nos. of Tunes.
Adeste fideles	81	47
Ah! dearest Lord! I cannot pray	63	63
Alas! o'er Erin's lessening shores	76	60
All hail! dear Conqueror! all hail!	13	27
All praise to St. Patrick, who brought to our mountains	50	50
All ye who love the ways of sin	46	18
Ave maris stella	85	73
Blest is the Faith, divine and strong	68	55
Christians! to the war	69	67
Come, Holy Ghost, Creator, come!	6	24
Come, Holy Spirit! from the height	7	43
Daily, daily, sing to Mary	35	6
Day breaks on temple-roofs and towers	24	64
Day set on Rome: its golden morn	47	45
Dear Angel! ever at my side	40	59
Dear Father Philip! holy Sire!	43	62, 63
Dear Husband of Mary! dear Nurse of her Child!	36	26
Dear Little One! how sweet Thou art	9	15
De profundis clamavi ad te, Domine	89	74
Faith of our Fathers! living still	55	14
Faith of our Fathers! living still (for Ireland)	56	14
Fountain of Love! Thyself true God!	5	2
From pain to pain, from woe to woe	86	68
God of Mercy! let us run	27	12
Hail, bright Archangel! Prince of heaven!	38	65
Hail, Gabriel! hail! a thousand hails	39	46
Hail! holy Joseph, hail!	37	9
Hail! holy Wilfrid, hail!	51	35
Hail, Jesus! hail! who for my sake	18	4
Hark! hark! my soul! angelic songs are swelling	67	51
Have mercy on us, God Most High!	1	1
Holy Ghost, come down upon Thy Children	8	57

INDEX.

	No of Hymn.	Nos. of Tunes.
How gently flow the silent years	48	65
How shalt thou bear the Cross, that now	58	64
How the light of heaven is stealing	64	59
It is no earthly summer's ray	41	78
I was wandering and weary	54	13, 79
Jesus, gentlest Saviour	20	58
Jesus is God! the solid earth	4	66
Jesus! my Lord, my God, my All!	16	17
Joy! joy! the Mother comes	26	20
Joy of my heart! O let me pay	30	48, 76
Like the dawning of the morning	25	7
Litany of Loretto	83	53
Magnificat anima mea Dominum	82	—
Miserere mei, Deus	88	75
Mother Mary! at thine altar	32	6, 7
Mother of Mercy! day by day	29	10
My God, how wonderful Thou art!	2	2
My God! who art nothing but mercy and kindness	60	22
Now are the days of humblest prayer	90	—
O blessed Father! sent by God	49	31
O come and mourn with me awhile	11	3, 8
O come to the merciful Saviour that calls you	59	29
O do you hear that voice from heaven	61	36
O Flower of Grace! divinest Flower!	31	21
O God! Thy power is wonderful	52	37
O happy Flowers! O happy Flowers!	19	30
O it is hard to work for God	57	62
O it is sweet to think	71	41
O Jesus! God and Man!	53	32
O Jesus, Jesus! dearest Lord!	3	23
O mighty Mother! why that light	15	2, 62, 63
O Mother! I could weep for mirth	23	33
O Paradise! O Paradise!	73	40
O purest of creatures! sweet Mother! sweet Maid!	21	11, 77
O salutaris Hostia	79	51, 71
O Soul of Jesus, sick to death	10	16
O turn to Jesus, Mother, turn	34	8
O what are the wages of sin	62	34
O what is this splendour that beams on me now	72	56
Saint of the Sacred Heart	42	35
Saint Philip! I have never known	45	28, 62, 63
Salve Regina, mater misericordiæ	84	—
Sing, sing, ye Angel Bands	28	20
Stabat Mater dolorosa	87	69
Sweet St. Philip! thou hast won us	44	5
Sweet Saviour! bless us ere we go	70	25

INDEX.

	No. of Hymn.	Nos. of Tunes.
Tantum ergo Sacramentum	80	52, 70
Te Deum laudamus: te Dominum confitemur	78	72
The chains that have bound me are flung to the wind	65	19
The day, the happy day, is dawning	22	—
The moon is in the heavens above	33	61
The world is wise, for the world is old	75	44
Thousands of years have come and gone	12	38
Unchanging and unchangeable, before angelic eyes	17	37
Veni Creator Spiritus	77	24
Who are these that ride so fast o'er the desert's sandy road	74	—
Why art thou sorrowful, servant of God	66	42
Why is thy face so lit with smiles	14	49, 63, 68

ADVERTISEMENT.

The present work is a collection of the Hymns and Sacred Songs, with the Tunes, used by the Congregation of the London Oratory in their Church and Oratory, and in the Schools of Compassion. The Second Part consists of a few Sacred Ballads for Schools, which for convenience have been printed with the Hymns. An Appendix has also been added, containing the Te Deum, and certain other Latin Hymns and Psalms, which may often be found useful in Novenas, Retreats, &c.

When the work was in the press, it was discovered that one or two of the tunes were copyright in this country, and therefore they have been unavoidably omitted. As so many inquiries were being made for the Hymn-book, it was thought better not to delay the publication by seeking for other tunes to supply their place; and a few pages of blank music-paper have been added at the end of the book, to enable those who wish it to enter in MS. these tunes, and any other additional tunes that may be found suitable to the Hymns.

ADVERTISEMENT.

The Editors have to apologise for a mistake, which was only observed when it was too late to correct it. The *Latin* words of the *Adeste Fideles* are given in the letterpress, while in the music the tune is printed with the *English* words. It is perhaps an error of no great importance, as the Hymn is generally sung in Latin.

CATHOLIC HYMNS.

1.

The Most Holy Trinity.

1 Have mercy on us, God Most High!
   Who lift our hearts to Thee;
 Have mercy on us worms of earth,
   Most Holy Trinity!

2 Most ancient of all mysteries!
   Before Thy throne we lie;
 Have mercy now, most merciful,
   Most Holy Trinity!

3 When Heaven and earth were yet unmade,
   When time was yet unknown,
 Thou in Thy bliss and majesty
   Didst live and love alone!

4 Thou wert not born, there was no fount
   From which Thy Being flowed;
 There is no end which Thou canst reach:
   But Thou art simply God.

5 How wonderful creation is!
   The work that Thou didst bless;
 And, oh! what then must Thou be like,
   Eternal Loveliness!

6 O Majesty most beautiful!
   Most Holy Trinity!
 On Mary's throne we climb to get
   A far-off sight of Thee.

7 Oh, listen, then, Most Pitiful!
    To Thy poor creature's heart;
  It blesses Thee that Thou art God,
    That Thou art what Thou art!

8 Most ancient of all mysteries!
    Still at Thy throne we lie;
  Have mercy now, most merciful,
    Most Holy Trinity!

2.

The Eternal Father.

1 My God, how wonderful Thou art!
    Thy Majesty how bright!
  How beautiful Thy Mercy-Seat
    In depths of burning light!

2 How dread are Thine eternal years,
    O everlasting Lord!
  By prostrate spirits day and night
    Incessantly adored!

3 How beautiful, how beautiful
    The sight of Thee must be,
  Thine endless wisdom, boundless power,
    And awful purity!

4 O how I fear Thee, Living God!
    With deepest, tenderest fears,
  And worship Thee with trembling hope
    And penitential tears.

5 Yet I may love Thee too, O Lord!
    Almighty as Thou art;
  For Thou hast stooped to ask of me
    The love of my poor heart.

6 No earthly father loves like Thee;
    No mother half so mild
  Bears and forbears, as Thou hast done
    With me Thy sinful child.

7 Only to sit and think of God,
   O what a joy it is!
To think the thought, to breathe the Name,
   Earth has no higher bliss!

8 Father of Jesus, love's Reward!
   What rapture will it be,
Prostrate before Thy Throne to lie,
   And gaze and gaze on Thee!

3.

Jesus, my God and my all.

1 O Jesus, Jesus! dearest Lord!
   Forgive me if I say
For very love Thy sacred Name
   A thousand times a day.

2 I love Thee so, I know not how
   My transports to control;
Thy love is like a burning fire
   Within my very soul.

3 O wonderful! that Thou shouldst let
   So vile a heart as mine
Love Thee with such a love as this,
   And make so free with Thine.

4 The craft of this wise world of ours
   Poor wisdom seems to me;
Ah! dearest Jesus! I have grown
   Childish with love of Thee.

5 For Thou to me art all in all,
   My honour and my wealth,
My heart's desire, my body's strength
   My soul's eternal health.

6 Burn, burn, O Love! within my heart,
   Burn fiercely night and day,
Till all the dross of earthly loves
   Is burned, and burned away.

7 O Light in darkness, Joy in grief,
   O Heaven begun on earth!
Jesus! my Love! my Treasure! who
   Can tell what Thou art worth?

8 O Jesus! Jesus! sweetest Lord!
   What art Thou not to me?
Each hour brings joys before unknown,
   Each day new liberty!

9 What limit is there to thee, love?
   Thy flight where wilt thou stay?
On! on! our Lord is sweeter far
   To-day than yesterday.

10 O love of Jesus! Blessed love!
   So will it ever be;
Time cannot hold thy wondrous growth
   No, nor eternity.

4.

Jesus is God.

1 Jesus is God! the solid earth,
   The ocean broad and bright,
The countless stars, like golden dust
   That strew the skies at night,
The wheeling storm, the dreadful fire,
   The pleasant, wholesome air,
The summer's sun, the winter's frost,
   His own creations were.

2 Jesus is God! the glorious bands
   Of golden angels sing
Songs of adoring praise to Him,
   Their Maker and their King.
He was true God in Bethlehem's crib,
   On Calvary's cross true God,
He who in Heaven eternal reigned,
   In time on earth abode.

3 Jesus is God! there never was
    A time when He was not:
Boundless, eternal, merciful,
    The Word the Sire begot!
Backward our thoughts through ages stretch,
    Onward through endless bliss,—
For there are two eternities,
    And both alike are His!

4 Jesus is God! alas! they say
    On earth the numbers grow
Who His Divinity blaspheme
    To their unfailing woe.
And yet what is the single end
    Of this life's mortal span,
Except to glorify the God
    Who for our sakes was man?

5 Jesus is God! let sorrow come,
    And pain, and every ill;
All are worth while, for all are means
    His glory to fulfil;
Worth while a thousand years of life
    To speak one little word,
If by our Credo we might own
    The Godhead of our Lord!

6 Jesus is God! O could I now
    But compass land and sea,
To teach and tell this single truth,
    How happy should I be!
O had I but an angel's voice
    I would proclaim so loud,—
Jesus, the good, the beautiful,
    Is everlasting God!

7 Jesus is God! If on the earth
    This blessed faith decays,
More tender must our love become,
    More plentiful our praise.
We are not angels, but we may
    Down in earth's corners kneel,
And multiply sweet acts of love,
    And murmur what we feel

5.

The Eternal Spirit.

1 FOUNTAIN of Love! Thyself true God!
　　Who through eternal days,
　From Father and from Son hast flowed
　　In uncreated ways!

2 O Majesty unspeakable!
　　O Person all divine!
　How in the Threefold Majesty
　　Doth Thy procession shine!

3 Proceeding, yet of equal age
　　With Those whose love Thou art;
　Proceeding, yet distinct, from Those
　　From whom Thou seem'st to part:

4 An undivided Nature, shared
　　With Father and with Son;
　A Person by Thyself; with them
　　Thy simple essence One!

5 I dread Thee, Unbegotten Love!
　　True God! Sole Fount of Grace!
　And now before Thy blessed throne
　　My sinful self abase.

6 Thou art a God of fire, that doth
　　Create while He consumes!
　A God of light, whose rays on earth
　　Darken where He illumes!

7 O Spirit, beautiful and dread!
　　My heart is fit to break
　With love of Thy humility
　　For us poor sinners' sake.

8 Thy love of Jesus I adore:
　　My comfort this shall be,
　That when I serve my dearest Lord
　　That service worships Thee!

6.

Veni Creator.

1 Come, Holy Ghost, Creator, come!
   The darkness of our minds illume;
   Thy children's hearts, O God, inspire,
   And lighten with celestial fire.

2 Thou that art named the Paraclete,
   The Gift of God, His Spirit sweet;
   The Living Fountain, Fire, and Love,
   And gracious Unction from above:

3 Of God's Right Hand the Finger Thou,
   Who dost Thy sevenfold grace bestow;
   True Promise of the Father, rich
   In gifts of tongues and various speech.

4 Enable with perpetual light
   The dulness of our blinded sight;
   Our hearts with heavenly love fulfil
   To walk Thy way, and do Thy will.

5 Stablish our weakness, and refresh
   With fortitude our fainting flesh:
   Keep far our foes, give peace at home:
   Where Thou art guide, no ill can come

6 Teach us to know the Father, Son,
   And Thee, of both, to be but One,
   That through the ages all along
   This faith may be love's endless song.

7 To God the Father laud and praise,
   And to the Son, whom He did raise,
   And to the Holy Spirit be,
   Now and for all eternity.

7.

Veni Sancte Spiritus.

1 Come, Holy Spirit! from the height
   Of heaven send down Thy blessed light!
   Come, Father of the friendless poor!

Giver of gifts, and Light of hearts,
Come with that unction which imparts
  Such consolations as endure.

2 The Soul's Refreshment and her Guest,
Shelter in heat, in labour Rest,
  The sweetest Solace in our woe!
Come, blissful Light! O come and fill,
In all Thy faithful, heart and will,
  And make our inward fervour glow.

3 Where Thou art, Lord! there is no ill,
For evil's self Thy light can kill:
  O let that light upon us rise!
Lord, heal our wounds and cleanse our stains,
Fountain of grace! and with thy rains
  Our barren spirits fertilise.

4 Bend with Thy fires our stubborn will,
And quicken what the world would chill,
  And homeward call the feet that stray:
Virtue's reward, and final grace,
The Eternal Vision face to face,—
  Spirit of Love! for these we pray.

5 Come, Holy Spirit! bid us live;
To those who trust Thy mercy give
  Joys that through endless ages flow:
Thy various gifts, foretastes of Heaven,
Those that are named Thy sacred Seven,
  On us, O God of love! bestow.

8.
Holy Ghost, come down upon Thy Children.

1 HOLY Ghost, come down upon Thy children,
  Give us grace, and make us Thine;
Thy tender fires within us kindle,
  Blessed Spirit! Dove Divine!
For all within us good and holy
  Is from Thee, Thy precious gift;
In all our joys, in all our sorrows,
  Wistful hearts to Thee we lift.
            Holy Ghost, &c.

2 For Thou to us art more than father,
   More than sister, in Thy love,
So gentle, patient, and forbearing,
   Holy Spirit! heavenly Dove!
                      Holy Ghost, &c

3 O we have grieved Thee, gracious Spirit!
   Wayward, wanton, cold are we;
And still our sins, new every morning,
   Never yet have wearied Thee.
                      Holy Ghost, &c

4 Dear Paraclete! how hast thou waited
   While our hearts were slowly turned!
How often hath Thy love been slighted,
   While for us it grieved and burned!
                      Holy Ghost, &c.

5 Now, if our hearts do not deceive us,
   We would take Thee for our Lord;
O dearest Spirit! make us faithful
   To Thy least and lightest word.
                      Holy Ghost, &c.

6 Ah! sweet Consoler, though we cannot
   Love Thee as Thou lovest us,
Yet if Thou deignst our hearts to kindle,
   They will not be always thus.
                      Holy Ghost, &c.

7 With hearts so vile how dare we venture,
   King of kings, to love Thee so?
And how canst Thou, with such compassion,
   Bear so long with things so low?
                      Holy Ghost, &c.

9.

The Infant Jesus.

1 DEAR Little One! how sweet Thou art,
   Thine eyes how bright they shine,
So bright, they almost seem to speak
   When Mary's look meets Thine!

2 How faint and feeble is Thy cry,
　　Like plaint of harmless dove,
　When Thou dost murmur in Thy sleep
　　Of sorrow and of love!

3 When Mary bids Thee sleep Thou sleep'st,
　　Thou wakest when she calls;
　Thou art content upon her lap,
　　Or in the rugged stalls.

4 Simplest of Babes! with what a grace
　　Thou dost Thy Mother's will!
　Thine infant fashions well betray
　　The Godhead's hidden skill.

5 When Joseph takes Thee in his arms,
　　And smooths Thy little cheek,
　Thou lookest up into his face
　　So helpless and so meek.

6 Yes! Thou art what Thou seem'st to be,
　　A thing of smiles and tears;
　Yet Thou art God, and heaven and earth
　　Adore Thee with their fears.

7 Yes! dearest Babe! those tiny hands,
　　That play with Mary's hair,
　The weight of all the mighty world
　　This very moment bear.

8 Art Thou, weak Babe, my very God?
　　O I must love Thee then,
　Love Thee, and yearn to spread Thy love
　　Among forgetful men.

10.

The Agony.

1 O Soul of Jesus, sick to death!
　Thy blood and prayer together plead!
　My sins have bowed Thee to the ground,
　As the storm * bows the feeble reed.

　　　* For singing, "As tempests bow"

2 Midnight—and still the oppressive load
  Upon Thy tortured Heart doth lie;
  Still the abhorred procession winds
  Before Thy Spirit's quailing eye.

3 Deep waters have come in, O Lord!
  All darkly on Thy Human Soul;
  And clouds of supernatural gloom
  Around Thee are allowed to roll.

4 The weight of the eternal wrath
  Drives over Thee with pressure dread;
  And forced upon the olive roots,
  In death-like sadness droops Thy Head.

5 Thy Spirit weighs the sins of men;
  Thy science fathoms all their guilt;
  Thou sickenest heavily at Thy Heart,
  And the pores open,—blood is spilt.

6 And Thou hast struggled with it, Lord!
  Even to the limit of Thy strength,
  While hours, whose minutes were as years,
  Slowly fulfilled their weary length.

7 And Thou hast shuddered at each act,
  And shrunk with an astonished fear,
  As if Thou couldst not bear to see
  The loathsomeness of sin so near.

8 Sin and the Father's anger, they
  Have made Thy lower nature faint:
  All, save the love within Thy Heart,
  Seemed for the moment to be spent.

Part II.

9 My God! My God! and can it be
  That I should sin so lightly now,
  And think no more of evil thoughts
  Than of the wind that waves the bough?

10 I sin, and heaven and earth go round,
  As if no dreadful deed were done,
  As if God's Blood had never flowed
  To hinder sin, or to atone.

11 I walk the earth with lightsome step,
   Smile at the sunshine, breathe the air,
   Do my own will, nor ever heed
   Gethsemane and Thy long prayer.

12 Shall it be alway thus, O Lord?
   Wilt thou not work this hour in me
   The grace Thy Passion merited,
   Hatred of self and love of Thee?

13 O by the pains of Thy pure love,
   Grant me the gift of holy fear;
   And give me of Thy Bloody Sweat
   To wash my guilty conscience clear!

14 Ever when tempted, make me see,
   Beneath the olive's moon-pierced shade,
   My God, alone, outstretched, and bruised,
   And bleeding, on the earth He made.

15 And make me feel it was my sin,
   As though no other sins there were,
   That was to Him who bears the world
   A load that He could scarcely bear!

11.

Jesus crucified.

Part I.

1 O COME and mourn with me awhile;
   See, Mary calls us to her side;
   O come and let us mourn with her:
   Jesus, our Love, is crucified!

2 Have we no tears to shed for Him,
   While soldiers scoff and Jews deride?
   Ah, look how patiently He hangs:
   Jesus, our Love, is crucified!

3 How fast His hands and feet are nailed;
   His Blessed Tongue with thirst is tied;
   His failing Eyes are blind with blood:
   Jesus, our Love, is crucified!

4 His Mother cannot reach His face;
  She stands in helplessness beside;
  Her heart is martyred with her Son's:
  Jesus, our Love, is crucified!

5 Seven times He spoke, seven words of love,
  And all three hours His silence cried
  For mercy on the souls of men
  Jesus, our Love, is crucified!

6 What was Thy crime, my dearest Lord?
  By earth, by heaven, Thou hast been tried,
  And guilty found of too much love:
  Jesus, our Love, is crucified!

Part II.

7 Found guilty of excess of love,
  It was Thine own sweet will that tied
  Thee tighter far than helpless nails:
  Jesus, our Love, is crucified!

8 Death came, and Jesus meekly bowed;
  His falling Eyes he strove to guide
  With mindful love to Mary's face:
  Jesus, our Love, is crucified!

9 O break, O break, hard heart of mine!
  Thy weak self-love and guilty pride
  His Pilate and His Judas were:
  Jesus, our Love, is crucified!

10 Come, take thy stand beneath the Cross,
   And let the Blood from out that Side
   Fall gently on thee drop by drop;
   Jesus, our Love is crucified!

11 A broken heart, a fount of tears,
   Ask, and they will not be denied;
   A broken heart love's cradle is:
   Jesus, our Love, is crucified!

12 O Love of God! O Sin of man!
   In this dread act your strength is tried;
   And victory remains with love,
   For He, our Love, is crucified!

12.
The Descent of Jesus to Limbus.

1 Thousands of years had come and gone,
    And slow the ages seemed to move
To those expectant souls that filled
    That prison-house of patient love.

2 It was a weary watch of theirs,
    But onward still their hopes would press
Captives they were, yet happy too
    In their contented weariness.

3 As noiseless tides the ample depths
    Of some capacious harbour fill,
So grew the calm of that dread place
    Each day with increase swift and still.

4 Sweet tidings there St. Joseph took;
    The Saviour's work had then begun,
And of His three-and-thirty years
    But three alone were left to run.

5 And Eve, like Joseph's shadow, hung
    About him wheresoe'er he went;
She lived on thoughts of Mary's child,
    Trembled with hope, and was content.

6 But see! how hushed the crowd of souls!
    Whence comes the light of upper day?
What glorious Form is this that finds
    Through central earth its ready way?

7 'Tis God! 'tis Man! the living Soul
    Of Jesus, beautiful and bright,
The first-born of created things,
    Flushed with a pure resplendent light.

8 'Twas Mary's child! Eve saw Him come;
    She flew from Joseph's haunted side,
And worshipped, first of all that crowd,
    The Soul of Jesus Crucified.

9 So after four long thousand years,
    Faith reached her end, and Hope her aim;
And from them, as they passed away,
    Love lit her everlasting flame!

13.
Jesus risen.

1 ALL hail! dear Conqueror! all hail!
  O what a victory is thine!
  How beautiful Thy strength appears,
  Thy crimson wounds how bright they shine!

2 Thou camest at the dawn of day;
  Armies of souls around Thee were,
  Blest spirits thronging to adore
  Thy Flesh, so marvellous, so fair.

3 The everlasting Godhead lay
  Shrouded within those Limbs Divine,
  Nor left untenanted one hour
  That Sacred Human Heart of Thine.

4 They worshipped Thee, those ransomed souls,
  With the fresh strength of love set free;
  They worshipped joyously, and thought
  Of Mary while they looked on Thee.

5 And Thou too, Soul of Jesus! Thou
  Towards that sacred Flesh didst yearn,
  And for the beatings of that Heart
  How ardently Thy love did burn!

6 They worshipped, while the beauteous Soul
  Paused by the Body's wounded Side:—
  Bright flashed the cave—before them stood
  The Living Jesus Glorified.

7 Down, down, all lofty things on earth,
  And worship Him with joyous dread!
  O Sin! thou art undone by love!
  O Death! thou art discomfited!

8 Ye Heavens, how sang they in your courts,
  How sang the angelic choirs that day,
  When from His tomb the imprisoned God,
  Like the strong sunrise, broke away!

9 O I am burning so with love,
  I fear lest I should make too free;
  Let me lie silent and adore
  Thy glorified Humanity.

D

10 Ah! now thou sendest me sweet tears;
   Fluttered with love, my spirits fail,—
   What shall I say? Thou know'st my heart;
   All hail! dear Conqueror! all hail!

14.
The Ascension.

1 Why is thy face so lit with smiles,
   Mother of Jesus! why?
   And wherefore is thy beaming look
   So fixed upon the sky?

2 From out thine overflowing eyes
   Bright lights of gladness part,
   As though some gushing fount of joy
   Had broken in thy heart.

3 Mother! how canst thou smile to-day?
   How can thine eyes be bright,
   When He, thy Life, thy Love, thine All,
   Hath vanished from thy sight?

4 His rising form on Olivet
   A summer's shadow cast;
   The branches of the hoary trees
   Drooped as the shadow passed.

5 And as He rose with all His train
   Of righteous souls around,
   His blessing fell into thine heart,
   Like dew into the ground.

6 The Feet which thou hast kissed so oft,
   Those living Feet, are gone;
   Mother! thou canst but stoop and kiss
   Their print upon the stone.

7 Yes! He hath left thee, Mother dear
   His throne is far above;
   How canst thou be so full of joy,
   When thou hast lost thy Love?

8 O surely earth's poor sunshine now
   To thee mere gloom appears,
   When He is gone who was its light
   For three-and-thirty years.

9 Why do not thy sweet hands detain
   His Feet upon their way?
O why doth not the Mother speak
   And bid her Son to stay?

10 Ah no! thy love is rightful love,
   From all self-seeking free;
The change that is such gain to Him
   Can be no loss to thee!

15.

The Descent of the Holy Ghost.

1 O mighty Mother! why that light
   In thine uplifted eye?
Why that resplendent look of more
   Than queenlike majesty?

2 O waitest thou in this thy joy
   For Gabriel once again?
Is heaven about to part, and make
   The Blessed Vision plain?

3 She sat; beneath her shadow were
   The Chosen of her Son;
Within each heart and on each face
   Her power and spirit shone.

4 Queen of the Church! around thee shines
   The purest light of heaven,
And all created things to thee
   For thy domain are given!

5 Why waitest thou then, so abashed,
   Wrapt in extatic fear,
Speechless with adoration, hushed,—
   Hushed as though God were near?

6 She is a creature! See! she bows,
   She trembles though so great;—
Created Majesty o'erwhelmed
   Before the Increate!

7 He comes! He comes! That mighty Breath
   From heaven's eternal shores;
His uncreated freshness fills
   His Bride as she adores.

8 Earth quakes before that rushing blast,
   Heaven echoes back the sound,
  And mightily the tempest wheels
   That upper room around.

9 One moment—and the Spirit hung
   O'er her with dread desire;
  Then broke upon the heads of all
   In cloven tongues of fire.

10 Who knows in what a sea of love
    Our Lady's heart He drowned?
   Or what new gifts He gave her then?
    What ancient gifts he crowned?

11 Grace was so multiplied on her,
    So grew within her heart,
   She stands alone, earth's miracle,
    A being all apart.

12 What gifts He gave those chosen men,
    Past ages can display;
   Nay, more, their vigour still inspires
    The weakness of to-day.

13 O let us fall and worship Him,
    The Love of Sire and Son,
   The Consubstantial Breath of God,
    The Coeternal One!

16.
Corpus Christi.

1 Jesus! my Lord, my God, my all!
  How can I love Thee as I ought?
And how revere this wondrous gift,
  So far surpassing hope or thought?
    Sweet Sacrament! we Thee adore!
    O, make us love Thee more and more!

2 Had I but Mary's sinless heart
  To love Thee with, my dearest King!
O with what bursts of fervent praise
  Thy goodness, Jesus, would I sing!
    Sweet Sacrament! we Thee adore!
    O, make us love Thee more and more!

3 O see! within a creature's hand
    The vast Creator deigns to be,
Reposing infant-like, as though
    On Joseph's arm, or Mary's knee.
        Sweet Sacrament! we Thee adore!
        O, make us love Thee more and more!

4 Thy Body, Soul, and Godhead, all!
    O mystery of love divine!
I cannot compass all I have,
    For all Thou hast and art are mine!
        Sweet Sacrament! we Thee adore!
        O, make us love Thee more and more!

5 Sound, sound His praises higher still,
    And come, ye angels, to our aid,
'Tis God! 'tis God! the very God,
    Whose power both man and angels made!
        Sweet Sacrament! we Thee adore!
        O, make us love Thee more and more!

6 Ring joyously, ye solemn bells!
    And wave, O wave, ye censers bright!
'Tis Jesus cometh, Mary's Son,
    And God of God, and Light of Light!
        Sweet Sacrament! we Thee adore!
        O, make us love Thee more and more!

7 O earth! grow flowers beneath His feet,
    And thou, O sun, shine bright this day!
He comes! He comes! O Heaven on earth!
    Our Jesus comes upon His way!
        Sweet Sacrament! we Thee adore!
        O, make us love Thee more and more!

8 He comes! He comes! the Lord of Hosts,
    Borne on His throne triumphantly!
We see Thee, and we know Thee, Lord;
    And yearn to shed our blood for Thee.
        Sweet Sacrament! we Thee adore!
        O, make us love Thee more and more!*

9 Our hearts leap up; our trembling song
    Grows fainter still; we can no more;

* Verses 6, 7, 8 are usually omitted in singing.

Silence! and let us weep—and die
Of very love, while we adore.
Great Sacrament of love divine!
All, all we have or are be Thine!

17.

The Sacred Heart.

1 Unchanging and unchangeable, before angelic eyes,
The Vision of the Godhead in its tranquil beauty lies;
And like a city lighted up all gloriously within,
Its countless lustres glance and gleam, and sweetest worship win.
On the Unbegotten Father, awful well-spring of the Three,
On the Sole Begotten Son's coequal Majesty,
On Him eternally breathed forth from Father and from Son,
The spirits gaze with fixed amaze, and unreckoned ages run.

2 Still the Fountain of the Godhead giveth forth eternal Being,
Still begetting, still begotten, still His own perfection seeing,
Still limiting His own loved Self with His dear coequal Spirit,
No change comes o'er His blissful Life, no shadow passeth near it.
And beautiful dread Attributes, all manifold and bright,
Now thousands seem, now lose themselves in one self-living light;
And far in that deep Life of God, in harmony complete,
Like crownèd kings, all opposite perfections take their seat.

3 See! deep within the glowing depth of that Eternal Light,
What change hath come, what vision new transports angelic sight?
A creature can it be, in uncreated bliss?
A novelty in God? O what nameless thing is this?
The beauty of the Father's Power is o'er it brightly shed,
The sweetness of the Spirit's Love is unction on its head;
In the wisdom of the Son it plays its wondrous part,
While it lives the loving life of a real Human Heart!

4 A Heart that hath a Mother, and a treasure of red Blood,
A Heart that man can pray to, and feed upon for food!
In the brightness of the Godhead is its marvellous abode,
A change in the Unchanging, Creation touching God!
Ye spirits blest, in endless rest, who on that Vision gaze,
Salute the Sacred Heart with all your worshipful amaze,
And adore, while with extatic skill the Three in One ye scan,
The Mercy that hath planted there that blessed Heart of Man!

5 All tranquilly, all tranquilly, doth that Blissful Vision last,
And Its brightness o'er immortalised creation will it cast;
Ungrowing and unfading, Its pure Essence doth it keep,
In the deepest of those depths where all are infinitely deep;
Unchanging and unchangeable as It hath ever been,

As It was before that Human Heart was there
  by angels seen,
So is It at this very hour, so will It ever be,
With that Human Heart within It, beating
  hot with love of me!

18.

The Precious Blood.

(FROM THE ITALIAN.)

1 HAIL, Jesus! hail! who for my sake
    Sweet Blood from Mary's veins didst take,
      And shed it all for me;
    O blessed be my Saviour's Blood,
    My life, my light, my only good,
      To all eternity.

2 To endless ages let us praise
    The Precious Blood, whose price could raise
      The world from wrath and sin;
    Whose streams our inward thirst appease,
    And heal the sinner's worst disease,
      If he but bathe therein.

3 O sweetest Blood, that can implore
    Pardon of God, and heaven restore,
      The heaven which sin had lost:
    While Abel's blood for vengeance pleads,
    What Jesus shed still intercedes
      For those who wrong Him most.

4 Oh, to be sprinkled from the wells
    Of Christ's own Sacred Blood, excels
      Earth's best and highest bliss:
    The ministers of wrath divine
    Hurt not the happy hearts that shine
      With those red drops of His!

5 Ah! there is joy amid the Saints,
    And hell's despairing courage faints
      When this sweet song we raise:

O louder then, and louder still,
Earth with one mighty chorus fill,
The Precious Blood to praise!

To all the faithful who say or sing the above Hymn, Pius VII. grants an indulgence of 100 days: applicable also to the souls in purgatory.

19.

Communion.

1 O HAPPY Flowers! O happy Flowers!
How quietly for hours and hours,
In dead of night, in cheerful day,
Close to my own dear Lord you stay,
Until you gently fade away!
O happy Flowers, what would I give
In your sweet place all day to live,
And then to die, my service o'er,
Softly as you do, at His door.

2 O happy Lights! O happy Lights!
Watching my Jesus livelong nights,
How close you cluster round His throne,
Dying so meekly one by one,
As each its faithful watch has done.
Could I with you but take my turn,
And burn with love of Him, and burn
Till love had wasted me, like you—
Sweet lights! what better could I do?

3 O happy Pyx! O happy Pyx!
Where Jesus doth His dwelling fix;
O little palace, dear and bright,
Where He, who is the world's true light,
Spends all the day, and stays all night!
Ah! if my heart could only be
A little home for Him like thee,
Such fires my happy soul would move,
I could not help but die of love!

4 O Pyx, and Lights, and Flowers! but I
Through envy of you will not die:

Nay, happy things! what will you do,
For I am better off than you,
The whole day long, the whole night through!
For Jesus gives Himself to me,
So sweetly and so utterly,
By rights long since I should have died
For love of Jesus Crucified.

5 My happy Soul! my happy Soul!
How shall I then my love control?
O sweet Communion! Feast of bliss!
When the dear Host my tongue doth kiss,
What happiness is like to this?
O heaven, I think, must be alway
Quite like a First Communion Day;
With love so sweet and joy so strange,—
Only that heaven will never change!

20.

Thanksgiving after Communion.

1 Jesus, gentlest Saviour!
   God of might and power!
Thou Thyself art dwelling
   In us at this hour.

2 Nature cannot hold Thee,
   Heaven is all too strait
For Thine endless glory
   And Thy royal state.

3 Out beyond the shining
   Of the furthest star,
Thou art ever stretching
   Infinitely far.

4 Yet the hearts of children
   Hold what worlds cannot,
And the God of wonders
   Loves the lowly spot.

5 As men to their gardens
   Go to seek sweet flowers,
In our hearts dear Jesus
   Seeks them at all hours.

6 Jesus, gentlest Saviour!
 Thou art in us now;
Fill us full of goodness
 Till our hearts o'erflow.

7 Pray the prayer within us
 That to heaven shall rise;
Sing the song that angels
 Sing above the skies.

8 Multiply our graces,
 Chiefly love and fear,
And, dear Lord! the chiefest—
 Grace to persevere.

9 Oh, how can we thank Thee
 For a gift like this,
Gift that truly maketh
 Heaven's eternal bliss.

10 Ah! when wilt Thou always
 Make our hearts Thy home?
We must wait for Heaven,—
 Then the day will come.

11 Now at least we'll keep Thee
 All the time we may—
But Thy grace and blessing
 We will keep alway.

12 When our hearts Thou leavest,
 Worthless though they be,
Give them to Thy Mother
 To be kept for Thee.

21.

The Immaculate Conception.
PART I.

1 O PUREST of creatures! sweet Mother! sweet Maid!
The one spotless womb wherein Jesus was laid!
Dark night hath come down on us, Mother! and we
Look out for thy shining, sweet Star of the Sea!

2 Deep night hath come down on this rough-spoken world,
 And the banners of darkness are boldly unfurled;
 And the tempest-tossed Church—all her eyes are on thee,
 They look to thy shining, sweet Star of the Sea!

3 The Church doth what God had first taught her to do;
 He looked o'er the world to find hearts that were true;
 Through the ages He looked, and He found none but thee,
 And He loved thy clear shining, sweet Star of the Sea!

4 He gazed on thy soul; it was spotless and fair;
 For the empire of sin—it had never been there;
 None had e'er owned thee, dear Mother! but He,
 And He blessed thy clear shining, sweet Star of the Sea!

5 Earth gave Him one lodging; 'twas deep in thy breast,
 And God found a home where the sinner finds rest;
 His home and His hiding-place, both were in thee,
 He was won by thy shining, sweet Star of the Sea!

6 O blissful and calm was the wonderful rest
 That thou gavest thy God in thy virginal breast;
 For the heaven He left He found heaven in thee,
 And He shone in thy shining, sweet Star of the Sea!

PART II.

7 To sinners what comfort, to angels what mirth,
   That God found one creature unfallen on earth,
   One spot where His Spirit untroubled could be,
   The depths of thy shining, sweet Star of the Sea!

8 So age after age in the Church had gone round,
   And the Saints new inventions of homage have found,
   New titles of honour, new honours for thee,
   New love for thy shining, sweet Star of the Sea!

9 And now from the Church of all lands thy dear name
   Comes borne on the breath of one mighty acclaim;
   Men call on their father that he should decree
   A new gem to thy shining, sweet Star of the Sea!

10 O shine on us brighter than ever, then, shine!
   For the primest of honours, dear Mother! is thine;
   "Conceived without sin," thy new title shall be,
   Clear light from thy birth-spring, sweet Star of the Sea!

11 So worship we God in these rude latter days;
   So worship we Jesus our Love, when we praise
   His wonderful grace in the gifts He gave thee,
   The gift of clear shining, sweet Star of the Sea!

12 Deep night hath come down on us, Mother! deep night,
   And we need more than ever the guide of thy light;
   For the darker the night is, the brighter should be
   Thy beautiful shining, sweet Star of the Sea!

22.

Sine Labe Originali Concepta.

1 THE day, the happy day, is dawning,
  The glorious feast of Mary's chiefest praise,
 That brightens, like a second morning,
  The clouded evening of these latter days.
   O every clime! O every nation!
   Praise, praise the God of our salvation!

2 High up, the realm of angels ringeth
  With hymns of triumph to its mortal queen,
 While earth its song of welcome singeth
  In every shady grove and valley green.
   O every clime! &c.

3 Hail Queen, whose life is just beginning,
  Thrice welcome, Mother of a fallen race,
 The sinless come to save the sinning,
  Thyself the chosen aqueduct of grace.
   O every clime! &c.

4 Immaculate! O dear exemption,
  A spotless soul for God, entire and free.
 Redeemed with such a choice redemption,
  Angel nor saint can share the praise with thee.
   O every clime! &c.

5 O virgin brighter than the brightest
  'Mid all the beauteous throngs that shine above!
 O maiden whiter than the whitest
  Of lily flowers in Eden's sacred grove!
   O every clime! &c.

6 Chief miracle of God's compassion,
  Choice mirror of His burning holiness,
 Whose heart His mercy deigned to fashion
  Far more than Eva's ruin to redress.
   O every clime! &c.

7 Earth's cities! let your bells be reeling,
  And all your temple-gates wide open fling,
 With banners flying, cannon pealing,
  The blessed Queen of our Redemption sing.
   O every clime! &c.

8 See! Mary comes! O jubilation!
   She comes with love to cheer a guilty race;
  O triumph! triumph all Creation
   O Christians! triumph in redeeming grace.
    O every clime! &c.

23.

Immaculate! Immaculate!

THE FEAST OF THE IMMACULATE CONCEPTION.

1 O MOTHER! I could weep for mirth,
  Joy fills my heart so fast;
My soul to-day is heaven on earth,
  O could the transport last!
    I think of thee, and what thou art,
      Thy majesty, thy state;
    And I keep singing in my heart,—
      Immaculate! Immaculate!

2 When Jesus looks upon thy face,
  His Heart with rapture glows,
And in the Church, by His sweet grace,
  Thy blessed worship grows.
    I think of thee, &c.

3 The angels answer with their songs,
  Bright choirs in gleaming rows;
And saints flock round thy feet in throngs,
  And heaven with bliss o'erflows.
    I think of thee, &c.

4 O, I would rather, Mother dear!
  Thou shouldst be what thou art,
Than sit where thou dost, O so near
  Unto the Sacred Heart.
    I think of thee, &c.

5 O I would forfeit all for thee,
  Rather than thou shouldst miss
One jewel from thy majesty,
  One glory from thy bliss.
    I think of thee, &c.

6 Ah! I could die with such a sense,
    It were but loss to live,
If I could die in dear defence
    Of this prerogative.
        I think of thee, &c.

7 Conceived, conceived Immaculate!
    O what a joy for thee!
Conceived, conceived Immaculate!
    O greater joy for me!
        I think of thee, &c.

8 It is this thought to-day that lifts
    My happy heart to heaven,
That for our sakes thy choicest gifts
    To thee, dear Queen! were given.
        I think of thee, &c.

9 The glory that belongs to thee
    Seems rather mine than thine,
While all the cares that harass me
    Are rather thine than mine.
        I think of thee, &c.

10 O blessed be the Eternal Son,
    Who joys to call thee mother,
And let's poor men by sin undone
    For thy sake call Him brother,
        I think of thee, &c.

11 Immaculate Conception! far
    Above all graces blest!
Thou shinest like a royal star
    On God's Eternal Breast!
        I think of thee, &c.

12 God prosper thee, my Mother dear!
    God prosper thee, my Queen!
God prosper His own glory here,
    As it hath ever been!
        I think of thee, &c.

24.

Our Lady's Presentation.

1 Day breaks on temple-roofs and towers;
The city sleeps, the palms are still;
The fairest far of earth's fair flowers
    Mounts Sion's sacred hill.

2 O wondrous Babe! O child of grace!
The Holy Trinity's delight!
Sweetly renewing man's lost race,
    How fair Thou art, how bright!

3 Not all the vast angelic choirs,
That worship round the eternal throne,
With all their love can match the fires
    Of thy one heart alone.

4 Since God created land and sea,
No love hath been so like divine;
For none was ever like to thee,
    Nor worship like to thine.

5 Angels in Heaven, and souls on earth,
Thousands of years their songs may raise,
Nor equal thee, for thine was worth
    All their united praise.

6 Not only was thy heart above
All heaven and earth could e'er attain,—
Thou gavest it with so much love,
    'Twas worth as much again.

7 O Maiden most immaculate!
Make me to choose thy better part;
And give my Lord, with love as great,
    An undivided heart.

8 Would that my heart, dear Lord! were true,
Royal and undefiled and whole,
Like hers from whom Thy sweet love took
    The Blood to save my soul.

9 If here our hearts grudge aught to Thee,—
In that bright land beyond the grave,
We'll worship thee with souls set free,
    And give as Mary gave.

25.

Our Lady's Expectation.

1 Like the dawning of the morning
  On the mountain's golden heights,
Like the breaking of the moonbeams
  On the gloom of cloudy nights,
Like a secret told by angels,
  Getting known upon the earth,
Is the Mother's Expectation
  Of Messiah's speedy birth!

2 Thou wert happy, blessed Mother!
  With the very bliss of heaven,
Since the angel's salutation
  In thy raptured ear was given;
Since the Ave of that midnight,
  When thou wert anointed Queen,
Like a river overflowing
  Hath the grace within thee been.

3 On the mountains of Judea,
  Like the chariot of the Lord,
Thou wert lifted in thy spirit
  By the uncreated Word;
Gifts and graces flowed upon thee
  In a sweet celestial strife,
And the growing of thy Burden
  Was the lightening of thy life.

4 And what wonders have been in thee
  All the day and all the night,
While the Angels fell before thee,
  To adore the Light of Light.
While the glory of the Father
  Hath been in thee as a home,
And the sceptre of creation
  Hath been wielded in thy womb.

5 And the sweet strains of the psalmist
  Were a joy beyond control,
And the visions of the prophets
  Burnt like transports in thy soul;

But the Burden that was growing,
     And was felt so tenderly,
   It was Heaven, it was Heaven,
     Come before its time to thee.

6 O the feeling of thy Burden,
    It was touch and taste and sight;
  It was newer still and newer,
    All those nine months, day and night.
  Like a treasure unexhausted,
    Like a vision unconfess'd,
  Like a rapture unforgotten,
    It lay ever at thy breast.

7 Every moment did that Burden
    Press upon thee with new grace;
  Happy Mother! thou art longing
    To behold the Saviour's Face!
  O, His Human Face and Features
    Must be passing sweet to see;
  Thou hast seen them, happy Mother!
    O, then, show them now to me.

8 Thou hast waited, Child of David!
    And thy waiting now is o'er!
  Thou hast seen Him, Blessed Mother!
    And wilt see Him evermore!
  O, His Human Face and Features,
    They were passing sweet to see:
  Thou beholdest them this moment;
    Mother, show them now to me!

26.

The Purification.

Joy! joy! the Mother comes,
  And in her arms she brings
The Light of all the world,
  The Christ, the King of kings;
And in her heart the while
  All silently she sings.

2 St. Joseph follows near,
    In rapture lost and lorn,

While angels round about
　　　　In glowing circles move,
　　　And o'er the Mother broods
　　　　The Everlasting Dove.

3　There in the temple court
　　　Old Simeon's heart beats high,
　　And Anna feeds her soul
　　　With food of prophecy;
　　But, see! the shadows pass,
　　　The world's true Light draws nigh.

4　O Infant God! O Christ!
　　　O Light most beautiful!
　　Thou comest, Joy of Joys!
　　　All darkness to annul;
　　And brightest lights of earth
　　　Beside Thy Light are dull.

5　O Mary! bear Him quick
　　　Into His temple-gate,
　　For poor impatient souls
　　　His healing sunrise wait;
　　And pay His price, that He
　　　May be emancipate.

6　Yes! thou wilt set Him free;
　　　He will be wholly ours,
　　To lighten every soul
　　　In earth's benighted bowers,
　　Undoing Adam's curse,
　　　And turning thorns to flowers.

7　Ah! with what thrills of awe
　　　The Mother's heart is teeming,
　　To think the new-born Light,
　　　That o'er the world is streaming,
　　At His own Mother's hands
　　　Should stoop to need redeeming.

8　Then to that Mother now
　　　All rightful worship be!
　　For thou hast ransomed Him
　　　Who first did ransom thee;
　　O, with thy Mother's tongue
　　　Pray Him to ransom me!

27.

The Dolours of Our Lady.

1 GOD of Mercy! let us run
    Where yon fount of sorrows flows;
Pondering sweetly, one by one,
    Jesu's wounds and Mary's woes.

2 Ah! those tears Our Lady shed,
    Enough to drown a world of sin;
Tears that Jesu's sorrows fed,
    Peace and pardon well may win!

3 His five Wounds a very home
    For our prayers and praises prove;
And our Lady's Woes become
    Endless joys in Heaven above.

4 Jesus, who for us didst die,
    All on Thee our love we pour;
And in the Holy Trinity
    Worship Thee for evermore.
        (From the *Breviary*, "Summæ Deus Clementiæ.")

28.

The Assumption.

1 SING, sing, ye Angel Bands,
    All beautiful and bright;
For higher still, and higher,
    Through fields of starry light,
Mary, your Queen, ascends,
    Like the sweet moon at night.

2 A fairer flower than she
    On earth hath never been;
And, save the Throne of God,
    Your heavens have never seen
A wonder half so bright
    As your ascending Queen.

3 O happy Angels! look,
   How beautiful she is!
See! Jesus bears her up,
   Her hand is locked in His;
O who can tell the height
   Of that fair Mother's bliss?

4 And shall I lose thee then,
   Lose my sweet right to thee?
Ah, no! the Angels' Queen
   Man's mother still will be;
And thou, upon thy throne,
   Wilt keep thy love for me.

5 On, then, dear Pageant, on!
   Sweet music breathes around;
And love, like dew, distils
   On hearts in rapture bound;
The Queen of heaven goes up
   To be proclaimed and crowned!

6 On! through the countless stars
   Proceeds the bright army;
And Love Divine comes forth
   To light her on her way,
Through the short gloom of night
   Into celestial day.

7 The Eternal Father calls
   His daughter to be blessed;
The Son His Maiden-Mother
   Woos unto His Breast;
The Holy Ghost His spouse
   Beckons into her rest.

8 Swifter and swifter grows
   That marvellous flight of love,
As though her heart were drawn
   More vehemently above;
While jubilant angels part
   A pathway for the Dove!

9 Hark! hark! through highest heaven
   What sounds of mystic mirth!

Mary, by God proclaimed
  Queen of Immaculate Birth,
And diademed with stars,
  The lowliest of the earth!

10 See! see! the Eternal Hands
  Put on her radiant crown,
And the sweet Majesty
  Of Mercy sitteth down,
For ever and for ever,
  On her predestined throne!

29.

To our Blessed Lady.

1 Mother of Mercy! day by day
  My love of thee grows more and more;
Thy gifts are strewn upon my way
  Like sands upon the great sea-shore.

2 Though poverty and work and woe
  The masters of my life may be,
When times are worst, who does not know
  Darkness is light with love of thee?

3 But scornful men have coldly said
  Thy love was leading me from God;
And yet in this I did but tread
  The very path my Saviour trod.

4 They know but little of thy worth
  Who speak these heartless words to me;
For what did Jesus love on earth
  One-half so tenderly as thee?

5 Get me the grace to love thee more;
  Jesus will give if thou wilt plead;
And, Mother! when life's cares are o'er,
  O I shall love thee then indeed!

6 Jesus, when His three hours were run,
  Bequeath'd thee from the cross to me;
And O! how can I love thy Son,
  Sweet Mother! if I love not thee?

30.

Month of May.

PIOUS ASPIRATIONS TO THE MOTHER OF GOD FOR EVERY DAY IN THE MONTH.

(*From the Italian.*)

1 Joy of my heart! O let me pay
 To thee thine own sweet month of May.

2 Mary! one gift I beg of thee,—
 My soul from sin and sorrow free.

3 Direct my wandering feet aright,
 And be thyself mine own true light.

4 Be love of thee the purging fire,
 To cleanse for God my heart's desire.

5 Mother! be love of thee a ray
 From Heaven, to show the heavenward way.

6 Mary! make haste thy child to win
 From sin, and from the love of sin.

7 Mother of God! let my poor love
 A mother's prayers and pity move.

8 O Mary, when I come to die,
 Be thou, thy spouse, and Jesus nigh.

9 When mute before the Judge I stand,
 My holy shield be Mary's hand.

10 O Mary! let no child of thine
 In hell's eternal exile pine.

11 If time for penance still be mine,
 Mother, the precious gift is thine.

12 Thou, Mary, art my hope and life,
 The starlight of this earthly strife.

13 O, for my own and others' sin,
 Do thou, who canst, free pardon win.

14 To sinners all, to me the chief,
 Send, Mother, send thy kind relief.

15 To thee our love and troth are given;
   Pray for us, pray, bright Gate of Heaven.

16 Sweet Day-Star! let thy beauty be
   A light to draw my soul to thee.

17 We love thee, light of sinners' eyes!
   O let thy prayer for sinners rise.

18 Look at us, Mother Mary! see
   How piteously we look to thee.

19 I am thy slave, nor would I be
   For worlds from this sweet bondage free.

20 Oh Jesus, Joseph, Mary, deign
   My soul in heavenly ways to train.

21 Sweet Stewardess of God, thy prayers
   We beg, who are God's ransomed heirs.

22 O Virgin-born! O Flesh Divine!
   Cleanse us, and make us wholly Thine.

23 Mary, dear Mistress of my heart,
   What thou wouldst have me do impart.

24 Thou, who wert pure as driven snow,
   Make me as thou wert here below.

25 O Queen of Heaven! obtain for me
   Thy glory there one day to see.

26 O then and there, on that bright day,
   To me thy womb's chaste Fruit display.

27 Mother of God! to me no less,
   Vouchsafe a mother's sweet caress.

28 Be love of thee, my whole life long,
   A seal upon my wayward tongue.

29 Write on my heart's most secret core
   The Five dear Wounds that Jesus bore.

30 O give me tears to shed with thee
   Beneath the Cross on Calvary.

31 One more request, and I have done:
   With love of thee and thy dear Son
   More let me burn, and more each day,
   Till love of self is burned away.

31.

Another Month of Mary.

MARY, THE FLOWER OF GOD.

1 O Flower of Grace! divinest Flower!
God's light thy life, God's love thy dower!
That all alone with virgin ray
Dost make in heaven eternal May,
Sweet falls the peerless dignity
Of God's eternal choice in thee!
    Mother dearest! Mother fairest!
    Maiden purest! Maiden rarest!
    Help of earth and joy of heaven!
    Love and praise to thee be given,
      Blissful Mother! blissful Maiden!

2 Choice Flower! that bloomest on the breast
Of Jesus, which is now thy rest,
As thine was once the chosen bed
Of His dear Heart and sacred Head:
O Mary! sweet it is to see
Thy Son's creation graced by thee!
    Mother dearest! &c.

3 O queenly Flower! enthroned above,
The trophy of Almighty love!
Ah me! how He hath hung thee round
With all love-tokens that abound
With God's own light, beyond the reach
Of angel song or mortal speech!
    Mother dearest! &c.

4 O Flower of God! divinest Flower!
Elected for His inmost bower!
Where angels come not, there art thou,
A crown of glory on thy brow;
While far below, all bright and brave.
Their gleamy palms the ransomed wave.
    Mother dearest! &c.

5 O bless thee for thy beauty, then,
Delight of angels, trust of men!

A sceptre unto thee is given,
Queen of the Sacred Heart! in heaven,
Like His who made, O blest decree!
Thee for Himself, all else for thee!
　　Mother dearest! &c.

6 O godlike creature! nigh to God!
In whom the Eternal Word abode!
The mirror of God's beauty thou!
On thee His dread perfections show
So palpably, men's hearts might faint
With an exceeding ravishment.
　　Mother dearest! &c.

7 Yet thou didst bloom on earth at first,
In meekness proved, in sorrow nursed;
And heaven must own its debt to earth,
Sweet Flower! for thy surpassing worth;
And angels, for their queen's dear sake,
Our road to thee more smooth shall make.
　　Mother dearest! &c.

8 O Help of Christians! mercy-laden!
O blissful Mother! blissful Maiden!
O Sinless! were it not for thee,
There were in faith no liberty
To hold that God could stoop so low,
Or love his sinful creatures so.
　　Mother dearest! &c.

9 O Mary! when we think of thee,
Our hearts grow light as light can be;
For thou hast felt as we have felt,
And thou hast knelt as we have knelt;
And so it is,—that utterly,
Mother of God! we trust in thee!
　　Mother dearest! &c.

32.

The Orphans' Consecration to Mary
(FOR NORWOOD.)

1 MOTHER Mary! at thine altar
　　We thy little daughters kneel;

With a faith that cannot falter,
   To thy goodness we appeal.
We are seeking for a mother
   O'er the earth so waste and wide,
And from off His Cross our Brother
   Points to Mary by His side.

2 We have seen thy picture often
   With thy little Babe in arms,
And it ever seemed to soften
   All our sorrows with its charms;
So we want thee for our Mother,
   In thy gentle arms to rest,
And to share with Him our Brother
   That sweet pillow on thy breast.

3 We have none but thee to love us
   With a Mother's fondling care;
And our Father, God above us,
   Bids us fly for refuge there.
All the world is dark before us,
   We must out into its strife;
If thy fondness watch not o'er us,
   O how sad will be our life!

4 So we take thee for our Mother,
   And we claim our right to be,
By the gift of our dear Brother,
   Babes and daughters unto thee;
And the orphan's consecration
   Thou wilt surely not despise,
From thy bright and lofty station
   Close to Jesus in the skies.

5 Mother Mary! to thy keeping
   Soul and body we confide,
Toiling, resting, waking, sleeping,
   To be ever at thy side;
Cares that vex us, joys that please us,
   Life and death we trust to thee;
Thou must make them all for Jesus,
   And for all eternity!

33.

Sweet Mother-Maid.

1 The moon is in the heavens above,
    And its light lies on the foamy sea;
So shines the star of Mary's love
    O'er this stormy scene of misery.
  Our hands to life's hard work are laid,
    But our hearts are thine,
      Sweet Mother-Maid!

2 O thou art bright as bright can be,
    And as bountiful as thou art bright;
And welcome is the thought of thee,
    As the fragrance of an eastern night.
      Our hands, &c.

3 Wide earth can give no place of rest,
    And for sorrow's tale it hath no ear;
But thou dost echo in thy breast
    Grief's loud cry, and suffering's silent tear.
      Our hands, &c.

4 We are no longer desolate,
    Though our sins have stricken us at heart;
Whom thou didst bear hath borne their weight,
    And thou wert His partner in the smart.
      Our hands, &c.

5 Calm as the blessed eye of God
    When it looks o'er all this world below,
He bids thee shed His peace abroad,
    With a secret balm for every woe.
      Our hands, &c.

6 By thee we gain, dear spotless Queen!
    Some vision of what our God must be;
And in thy glory His is seen,
    For He shows Himself when He shows thee.
      Our hands, &c.

34.

To our Blessed Lady,

FOR THE SOULS IN PURGATORY.

1 O TURN to Jesus, Mother, turn,
    And call Him by His tenderest names;
Pray for the holy souls that burn
    This hour amid the cleansing flames.

2 Ah! they have fought a gallant fight;
    In death's cold arms they persevered;
And after life's uncheery night
    The harbour of their rest is neared.

3 In pains beyond all earthly pains,
    Favourites of Jesus! there they lie,
Letting the fire wear out their stains.
    And worshipping God's purity.

4 Spouses of Christ they are, for He
    Was wedded to them by His blood;
And angels o'er their destiny
    In wondering adoration brood.

5 They are the children of thy tears;
    Then hasten, Mother! to their aid,
In pity think each hour appears
    An age while glory is delayed.

6 See, how they bound amid their fires,
    While pain and love their spirits fill;
Then with self-crucified desires
    Utter sweet murmurs, and lie still.

7 Ah me! the love of Jesus yearns
    O'er that abyss of sacred pain,
And as He looks His Bosom burns
    With Calvary's dear thirst again.

8 O Mary! let thy Son no more
    His lingering Spouses thus expect;
God's children to their God restore,
    And to the Spirit His elect.

9 Pray then, as thou hast ever prayed;
  Angels and Souls all look to thee;
God waits thy prayers, for He hath made
  Those prayers His law of charity.

35.

Hymn of St. Casimir to the Blessed Virgin Mary.

1 Daily, daily, sing to Mary,
    Sing, my soul, her praises due;
  All her feasts, her actions worship,
    With the heart's devotion true.
      Lost in wond'ring contemplation,
        Be Her Majesty confest:
      Call her Mother, call her Virgin,
        Happy Mother, Virgin blest.

2 She is mighty to deliver;
    Call her, trust her lovingly:
  When the tempest rages round thee,
    She will calm the troubled sea.
      Gifts of Heaven she has given,
        Noble lady! to our race:
      She, the Queen, who decks her subjects
        With the light of God's own grace.

3 Sing, my tongue, the Virgin's trophies,
    Who for us her Maker bore;
  For the curse of old inflicted,
    Peace and blessing to restore.
      Sing in songs of praise unending,
        Sing the world's majestic Queen:
      Weary not, nor faint in telling,
        All the gifts she gives to men.

4 All my senses, heart, affections,
    Strive to sound her glory forth:
  Spread abroad the sweet memorials
    Of the Virgin's priceless worth.
      Where the voice of music thrilling
        Where the tongue of eloquence,
      That can utter hymns beseeming
        All her matchless excellence?

5 All our joys do flow from Mary,
   All then join her praise to sing:
Trembling sing the Virgin Mother,
   Mother of our Lord and King.
     While we sing her awful glory,
       Far above our fancy's reach,
     Let our hearts be quick to offer
       Love the heart alone can teach.

Part II.

6 Holy Mary, we implore thee
   By thy purity divine:
Help us, bending here before thee,
   Help us truly to be thine.
     Thou, unfolding wide the portals
       Of the kingdom in the skies,
     Holy Virgin, hast to mortals
       Shown the land of paradise.

7 Thou, when deepest night infernal
   Had for ages shrouded man,
Gavest us that light eternal
   Promised since the world began.
     God in thee hath showered plenty
       On the hungry and the weak;
     Sending back the mighty empty,
       Setting up on high the meek.

8 Thine the province to deliver
   Souls that deep in bondage lie:
Thine to crush, and crush for ever,
   Life-destroying heresy.
     Thine to show that earthly pleasures,
       All the world's enchanting bloom,
     Are outrivalled by the treasures
       Of the glorious life to come.

9 Teach, oh! teach us, holy Mother,
   How to conquer every sin,
How to love and help each other,
   How the prize of life to win.
     Thou to whom a Child was given,
       Greater than the sons of men,
     Coming down from highest Heaven
       To create this world again.

10 Oh! by that Almighty Maker,
  Whom thyself a virgin bore;
  Oh! by thy supreme Creator,
    Linked with thee for evermore;
     By the hope thy name inspires;
      By our doom, reversed through thee;
    Help us, Queen of Angel choirs,
    Now and through eternity.

36.

The Patronage of St. Joseph.

1 DEAR Husband of Mary! dear Nurse of her Child!
Life's ways are full weary, the desert is wild;
Bleak sands are all round us, no home can we see;
Sweet Spouse of our Lady! we lean upon thee.

2 For thou to the pilgrim art Father and Guide,
And Jesus and Mary felt safe by thy side;
Ah! blessed Saint Joseph! how safe should I be,
Sweet Spouse of our Lady! if thou wert with me!

3 O blessed Saint Joseph! how great was thy worth,
The one chosen shadow of God upon earth;
The Father of Jesus, ah, then, wilt thou be,
Sweet Spouse of our Lady! a father to me?

4 Thou hast not forgotten the long dreary road,
When Mary took turns with thee, bearing thy God;
Yet light was that Burden, none lighter could be:
Sweet Spouse of our Lady! O canst thou bear me?

5 A cold thankless heart, and a mean love of ease,
   What weights, blessed Patron! more galling than these?
  My life, my past life, thy clear vision may see;
  Sweet Spouse of our Lady! O canst thou love me?

6 Ah! give me thy Burden to bear for a while;
   Let me kiss His warm lips, and adore His sweet smile;
  With her Babe in my arms, surely Mary will be,
  Sweet Spouse of our Lady! my pleader with thee!

7 When the treasures of God were unsheltered on earth,
   Safe keeping was found for them both in thy worth;
  O Father of Jesus! be father to me,
  Sweet Spouse of our Lady! and I will love thee!

8 God chose thee for Jesus and Mary! wilt thou
   Forgive a poor exile for choosing thee now?
  There is no Saint in Heaven I worship like thee:
  Sweet Spouse of our Lady! O deign to love me!

37.

Hymn to St. Joseph.

1 Hail! holy Joseph, hail!
  Husband of Mary, hail!
  Chaste as the lily flower
  In Eden's peaceful vale.

2 Hail! holy Joseph, hail!
  Father of Christ esteemed!
  Father be thou to those
  Thy Foster-Son redeemed.

3 Hail! holy Joseph, hail!
  Prince of the House of God,
  May His best graces be
  By thy sweet hands bestowed.

4 Hail! holy Joseph, hail!
  Comrade of angels, hail!
  Cheer thou the hearts that faint,
  And guide the steps that fail.

5 Hail! holy Joseph, hail!
  God's choice wert thou alone;
  To thee the Word made flesh
  Was subject as a Son.

6 Hail! holy Joseph, hail!
  Teach us our flesh to tame;
  And, Mary, keep the hearts
  That love thy husband's name

7 Mother of Jesus! bless,
  And bless, ye Saints on high,
  All meek and simple souls
  That to Saint Joseph cry.

38.

St. Michael.

1 Hail, bright Archangel! Prince of heaven!
    Spirit divinely strong!
  To whose rare merit hath been given
    To head the angelic throng!

2 Thine the first worship was, when gloom
    Through heaven's thinned ranks did move,
  Thus giving unto God the bloom
    Of young creation's love.

3 O trumpet-tongued! O beautiful!
    O force of the Most High!
  The blessed of the earth look dull
    Beside thy majesty.

4 First servant of the Ineffable!
   The first created eye
That ever, proved and perfect, fell
   On the dread Trinity!

5 O Michael! worship Him this night,
   The Father, Word, and Dove,
Renewing with strong act the might
   Of thy first marvellous love.

6 Praise to the Three, whose love designed
   Thee champion of the Lord;
Who first conceived thee in His mind,
   And made thee with His Word.

7 Who stooped from nothingness to raise
   A life like thine so high,
Beauty and being that should praise
   His love eternally!

39.

St. Gabriel.

1 HAIL, Gabriel! hail! a thousand hails
For thine whose music still prevails
   In the world's listening ear!
Angelic Word! sent forth to tell
How the Eternal Word should dwell
   Amid His creatures here!

2 Angel of Jesus! days gone by
Bore burdens of kind prophecy
   To quicken hope delayed;
Then, preluding with John's sweet name,
At length thy choicest music came
   Unto the Mother-Maid.

3 Voice of heaven's sweetness, uttered low,
Thy words like strains of music grow
   Upon the stilly night;
Clear echoes from the Mind of God,
Stealing through Mary's blest abode
   In pulses of delight.

4 O Voice! dear Voice! the ages hear
  That Hail of thine still lingering near,
    An unexhausted song;
  And still thou com'st with balmy wing,
  And O! thou seemest still to sing,
    Thine Ave to prolong.

5 O blessed Gabriel! Tongue of God!
  Sweet-spoken Spirit! thou hast showed
    To us the Word made Man;
  He bade thee break His silence here;
  The tale thou told'st in Mary's ear
    His coming scarce foreran.

6 Joseph and John were, like to thee,
  Chosen for Mary's custody,
    In her retired abode.
  O Gabriel! get us love like theirs,
  For her whose unremitting prayers
    Have gained us love of God!

7 Take up in Heaven for us thy part,
  And, singing to the Sacred Heart,
    Thy strains of rapture raise;
  And tune with endless Ave still
  The voices of the Blessed, and fill
    The Ear of God with praise!

40.

The Guardian Angel.

(FOR THE SCHOOL-CHILDREN)

1 DEAR Angel! ever at my side,
    How loving must thou be,
  To leave thy home in Heaven to guard
    A guilty wretch like me!

2 Thy beautiful and shining face
    I see not, though so near;
  The sweetness of thy soft low voice
    I am too deaf to hear.

3 I cannot feel thee touch my hand
    With pressure light and mild,
To check me, as my mother did
    When I was but a child.

4 But I have felt thee in my thoughts
    Fighting with sin for me;
And when my heart loves God, I know
    The sweetness is from thee.

5 And when, dear Spirit! I kneel down,
    Morning and night, to prayer,
Something there is within my heart
    Which tells me thou art there.

6 Yes! when I pray thou prayest too—
    Thy prayer is all for me;
But when I sleep, thou sleepest not,
    But watchest patiently.

7 But most of all I feel thee near,
    When, from the good priest's feet,
I go absolved, in fearless love,
    Fresh toils and cares to meet.

8 And thou in life's last hour wilt bring
    A fresh supply of grace,
And afterwards wilt let me kiss
    Thy beautiful bright face.

9 Ah me! how lovely they must be
    Whom God has glorified!
Yet one of them, O sweetest thought!
    Is ever at my side.

10 Then, for thy sake, dear Angel! now
    More humble will I be:
But I am weak; and when I fall,
    O weary not of me:

11 O weary not, but love me still,
    For Mary's sake, thy Queen;
She never tired of me, though I
    Her worst of sons have been.

12 She will reward thee with a smile;
    Thou know'st what it is worth!
 For Mary's smiles each day convert
    The hardest hearts on earth.

13 Then love me, love me, Angel dear!
    And I will love thee more;
 And help me when my soul is cast
    Upon the eternal shore.

41.

St. Peter and St. Paul.

1 It is no earthly summer's ray
    That sheds this golden brightness round,
 Crowning with heavenly light the day
    The Princes of the Church were crowned.

2 The blessed Seer, to whom were given
    The hearts of men to teach and school;
 And he that keeps the keys of heaven,
    For those on earth that own his rule;—

3 Fathers of mighty Rome! whose word
    Shall pass the doom of life or death,
 By humble cross and bleeding sword
    Well have they won their laurel wreath.

4 O happy Rome! made holy now
    By these two martyrs' glorious blood;
 Earth's best and fairest cities bow,
    By thy superior claims subdued.

5 For thou alone art worth them all,
    City of martyrs! thou alone
 Canst cheer our pilgrim hearts, and call
    The Saviour's sheep to Peter's throne.

6 All honour, power, and praise be given
    To Him who reigns in bliss on high,
 For endless, endless years in heaven,
    One only God in Trinity!

                              Amen.
      (From the *Breviary*, " Decora lux æterni
                tatis auream.")

42.

St. John the Evangelist.

1 SAINT of the Sacred Heart,
  Sweet teacher of the Word,
  Partner of Mary's woes,
  And favourite of thy Lord!

2 Thou to whom grace was given
  To stand when Peter fell;
  Whose heart could brook the Cross
  Of Him it loved so well!

3 We know not all thy gifts;
  But this Christ bids us see,
  That He who so loved all
  Found more to love in thee.

4 When the last evening came,
  Thy head was on His breast,
  Pillowed on earth, where now
  In Heaven the saints find rest.

5 Thy long fair hair hung down,
  His glance spoke love to thine,
  While love's meek freedom owned
  The human and divine.

6 His heart, with quickened love,
  Because His hour drew near,
  Now throbbed against thy head,
  Now beat into thine ear.

7 He nursed thee in his lap,
  He loved thee to make free;
  What Mary was to Him,
  He made Himself to thee.

8 God and His friend, so free
  To touch, to rest, to move,
  The angels wondering gazed,
  And envied human love.

9 Dear Saint! I stand far off,
  With vilest sins opprest;
  O may I dare, like thee,
  To lean upon His breast?

10 His touch could heal the sick,
  His voice could raise the dead;
  O that my soul might be
  Where He allows thy head.

11 The gifts He gave to thee
  He gave thee to impart;
  And I, too, claim with thee
  His Mother and His Heart!

12 O teach me, then, dear Saint!
  The secrets Christ taught thee;
  The beatings of His Heart,
  And how it beat for me!

43.

To our Holy Father and Blessed Founder, St. Philip Neri.

(FOR THE LITTLE ORATORY.)

1 DEAR Father Philip! holy Sire!
  We are poor sons of thine,
  Thy last and least,—then to our prayers
  A father's ear incline.

2 We wandered weeping heretofore
  For many a long, long day;
  But thou hast taught us how to mourn
  In thy more tender way:

3 To mourn that God of all His sons
  So little loved should be;
  To mourn that 'mid the world's cold hearts
  None were more cold than we;

4 To mourn, and yet to joy and love,
  With overflowing heart,
  And in thy school of Christian mirth
  To bear our humble part.

5 'Mid strife and change, cold hearts and tongues
  How much we owe to thee!
  This sunny service! who could dream
  Earth had such liberty.

6 Look at the crowds of this sweet land,
  Dear Father Philip! see
 How shepherdless they wander on,
  How lone, how hopelessly!

7 O make us sons of thine indeed,
  Fill us with thy true mirth,
 Thy strength of prayer, thy might of love,
  To change these hearts of earth.

8 Dear Father Philip! give to us
  Thy manners gay and free,
 Thy patient trust, thy plaint of prayer,
  Thy deep simplicity.

44.

St. Philip's Penitents.

1 SWEET Saint Philip! thou hast won us,
  Though our hearts were hard as stone;
 Sin had once well-nigh undone us,
  Now we live for God alone.
   Help in Mary! Joy in Jesus!
   Sin and Self no more shall please us!
   We are Philip's gift to God.

2 Sweet Saint Philip! we are weeping,
  Not for sorrow, but for glee;
 Bless thy converts bravely keeping
  To the bargain made with thee!
   Help in Mary! &c.

3 Sweet Saint Philip! old friends want us
  To be with them as before;
 And old times, old habits, haunt us,
  Old temptations press us sore.
   Help in Mary! &c.

4 Sweet Saint Philip! do not fear us;
  Get us firmness, get us grace;
 Only thou, dear Saint! be near us;
  We shall safely run the race!
   Help in Mary! &c.

5 Sweet Saint Philip! make us wary;
  Sin and Death are all around;
Bring us Jesus! bring us Mary!
  We shall conquer and be crowned!
    Help in Mary! &c.

Sweet Saint Philip! keep us humble,
  Make us pure as thou wert pure;
Strongest purposes will crumble,
  If we boast and make too sure.
    Help in Mary! &c.

7 Sweet Saint Philip! come and ease us
  Of the weary load we bear;
Put us in the Heart of Jesus,
  Dearest Saint! and leave us there
    Help in Mary! &c.

45.

St. Philip's Picture.

1 SAINT PHILIP! I have never known
  A Saint as I know thee;
For none have made their wills and ways
  So plain for men to see.
I live with thee; and in my toil
  All day thou hast thy part;
And then I come at night to learn
  Thy picture off by heart.

2 O what a prayer thy picture is!
  Was Jesus like to thee?
Whence hast thou caught that lovely look
  That preaches so to me?
Sermon and prayer thy picture is,
  And music to the eye;
Song to the soul, a song that sings
  Of whitest purity!

3 A blessing on thy name, dear Saint!
  Blessing from young and old,
Whom thou in Mary's gallant band
  Hast winningly enrolled!

If ever there were poor man's Saint,
   That very Saint art thou!
If ever time were fit for thee,
   Dear Saint! that time is now!

4 Philip! strange missioner thou art,
   Biding so still at home,
Content if with the evening star
   Souls to thy nets will come!
If ever spell could make hard work
   Profit and pastime be,
That spell is in thy coaxing ways,
   That magic is in thee.

5 Sweet-faced old Man! for so I dare,
   Saint though thou be on high,
To name thee, for thou temptest love
   By thy humility.
Sweet-faced old Man! what are thy wiles
   With which thou winnest men?
Art thou all saints within thyself?
   If not, what art thou then?

6 John's love of Mary thou hast got;
   Thy house is Mary's home;
And then thou hast Paul's love of souls
   With Peter's love of Rome.
Thy heart, that was so large and strong,
   It could not quiet bide;
O was it not like his that beats
   Within a wounded Side?

7 Saint of the over-worked and poor!
   Saint of the sad and gay!
Jesus and Mary be with those
   Who keep to thy true way!
O bless us, Philip! Saint most dear!
   Thine Oratory bless;
And gain for those who seek thee there
   The gift of holiness!

46.

St. Philip's Charity.

1 ALL ye who love the ways of sin,
 Come to St. Philip's feet, and learn
The baits that Jesus hath to win
 His truant children to return.
  All praise and thanks to Jesus be
  For sweet St. Philip's charity!

2 That Saint can do such things for you
 As your poor hearts would never dream;
For he can make the false world true,
 And penance life's best pleasure seem.
  All praise, &c.

3 His words, like gentlest dews, distil;
 His face is calm as summer's eve;
His look can tame the wildest will,
 And make the stoutest heart to grieve.
  All praise, &c.

4 He smiles; and evil habit fails
 To bind its victim as before;
Old sins drop off the soul like scales,
 Old wounds are healed, and leave no sore.
  All praise, &c.

5 His hand, with virgin fragrance fraught,
 The heart with painless pressure strains;
And with one touch, all evil thought,
 All worldly longing from it drains.
  All praise, &c.

6 He breathes on us; the spicy gale
 Of Araby is not more sweet;
He breathes new life in hearts that fail,
 New vigour into weary feet.
  All praise, &c.

7 His voice can raise the dead to life,
 So wonderful its accents are;
He speaks,—there is an end of strife,
 And of the soul's internal war.
  All praise, &c.

8 Come, sinners! ye need not forego
   Your portion of light-hearted mirth;
He came, unthought-of roads to show,
   And plant a paradise on earth.
     All praise, &c.

9 Come, try the Saint: his words are true;
   Give him your hearts; he gives you heaven;
He sets light penance, and will do
   The penance he himself hath given.
     All praise, &c.

47.

St. Philip's Death.

1 DAY set on Rome: its golden morn
  Had seen the world's Creator borne
    Around St. Peter's square;
Trembling and weeping all the way,
God's Vicar with his God that day
    Made pageant brave and rare!

2 O come to Father Philip's cell,
Rome's rank and youth, they know it well,
    Come ere the moment flies!
The feast hath been too much for him;
His heart is full, his eye is dim,
    And Rome's Apostle dies!

3 Come, O Creator Spirit! come,
Take Thine elect unto his home,
    Thy chosen one, sweet Dove!
"Come to thy rest," he hears Thee say
He waits not—he hath passed away
    In mortal trance of love.

4 When Rome in deepest slumber slept,
Our father's children knelt and wept
    Around his little bed;
He raised his eyes, then let them fall
With marked expression upon all;
    He blessed them and was dead.

5 One half from earth, one half from heaven,
  Was that mysterious blessing given;
    Just as his life had been
  One half in heaven, one half on earth,
  Of earthly toil and heavenly mirth
    A wondrous woven scene!

6 O Jesus, Mary, Joseph, bide,
  With kind St. Raphael, by my side,
    When death shall come for me;
  And, Philip! leave me not that day,
  But let my spirit pass away,
    Leaning, dear Sire, on thee!

48.

St. Martin and St. Philip.

Part I.

1 How gently flow the silent years,
    The seasons one by one!
  How sweet to feel each month that goes,
    That life must soon be done!

2 O weary ways of earth and men!
    O self more weary still!
  How vainly do you vex the heart
    That none but God can fill!

3 It is not weariness of life
    That makes us wish to die;
  But we are drawn by cords which come
    From out eternity.

4 Eye has not seen, ear has not heard,
    No heart of man can tell
  The store of joys God has prepared
    For those who love Him well.

5 O may those joys one day be ours,
    Upon that happy shore!
  And yet those joys are not enough—
    We crave for something more.

Part II.

6 The world's unkindness grows with life,
   And troubles never cease;
'Twere lawful, then, to wish to die,
   Simply to be at peace.

7 Yes! peace is something more than joy,
   Even the joys above;
For peace, of all created things,
   Is likest Him we love.

8 But not for joy, nor yet for peace,
   Dare we desire to die;
God's will on earth is always joy,
   Always tranquillity.

9 To die, that we might sin no more,
   Were scarce a hero's prayer;
And glory grows as grace matures,
   And patience loves to bear.

10 And yet we long and long to die,
   We covet to be free;
Not for thy great rewards, O God!
   Nor for Thy peace—but Thee!

11 O call not this a selfish love,
   A turning from the fight;
O tell us not, for others' sakes,
   To doubt if this be right.

12 If he were wanted for his Lord,
   St. Martin prayed to stay:
'Twas well; and yet it was a prayer
   St. Philip would not pray.

13 O leave us, then, at peace to greet
   Each waxing waning moon,
Whose silver light seems aye to say—
   Soon, exile spirit! soon!

49.

St. Vincent of Paul.

Part I.

1 O BLESSED Father! sent by God,
    His mercy to dispense,
 Thy hand is out o'er all the earth
    Like God's own providence.

2 There is no grief or care of men
    Thou dost not own for thine,
 No broken heart thou dost not fill
    With mercy's oil and wine.

3 Thy miracles are works of love;
    Thy greatest is to make
 Room in a day for toils, that weeks
    In other men would take.

4 All cries of suffering through the earth
    Upon thy mercy call,
 As though thou wert, like God Himself,
    A Father unto all.

5 Dear Saint! not in the wilderness
    Thy fragrant virtues bloom,
 But in the city's crowded haunts,
    The alley's cheerless gloom:

6 The Father of the childless old,
    The lonesome widow's stay,
 The gladness of the orphan groups
    Out in the streets at play.

7 Yet not unto the towns confined
    The gifts thy mercy gave,
 The gospel to the villager,
    His freedom to the slave.

8 So for the sake of timid souls,
    And love of winning ways,
 Thou didst against hard-hearted schools
    Thy gentle protest raise.

9 For charity anointed thee
   O'er want, and woe, and pain ;
And she hath crowned thee emperor
   Of all her wide domain.

Part II.

10 Vincent! like Mother Mary, thou
   Art no one's patron saint;
Eyes to the blind, health to the sick,
   And life to those who faint.

11 Of body and of soul alike
   Thou art physician wise,
And full of joy as if thou wert
   Raphael in mortal guise.

12 The poor thou savest by such charms
   As hardest hearts can move,—
The rich by teaching them to do
   The saving works of love.

13 Saint of wide-open arms, and heart
   Capacious as a sea,
In dead of night a thousand lips
   Are sweetly blessing thee:

14 In orphanage, in hospital,
   The sick on garret-bed,
The dying, and the desolate
   Who weep beside the dead.

15 Thou seem'st to have a thousand hands,
   And in each hand a heart;
And all the hearts a precious balm
   Like dew from God impart.

16 So thou belongest unto all,
   And all belong to thee;
And we in him Thy pity praise,
   Most Holy Trinity!

50.

St. Patrick's Day.

1 ALL praise to St. Patrick, who brought to our
 mountains
 The gift of God's faith, the sweet light of
 His love!
 All praise to the shepherd who showed us the
 fountains
 That rise in the Heart of the Saviour above!
 For hundreds of years,
 In smiles and in tears,
 Our saint hath been with us, our shield and
 our stay;
 All else may have gone,—
 St. Patrick alone—
 He hath been to us light when earth's lights
 were all set,
 For the glories of faith they can never decay;
 And the best of our glories is bright with us yet,
 In the faith and the feast of St. Patrick's Day

2 There is not a saint in the bright courts of
 heaven
 More faithful than he to the land of his
 choice;
 Oh, well may the nation to whom he was given,
 In the feast of their sire and apostle rejoice!
 In glory above,
 True to his love,
 He keeps the false faith from his children away:
 The dark false faith,
 Far worse than death—
 O he drives it far off from the green sunny
 shore,
 Like the reptiles which fled from his curse
 in dismay;
 And Erin, when error's proud triumph is o'er,
 Will still be found keeping St. Patrick's
 Day.

3 Then what shall we do for thee, heaven-sent
    father?
  What shall the proof of our loyalty be?
  By all that is dear to our hearts, we would
    rather
    Be martyred, sweet Saint! than bring shame
      upon thee!
      But oh! he will take
      The promise we make,
    So to live that our lives by God's help may
      display
      The light that he bore
      To Erin's shore:
Yes! Father of Ireland! no child wilt thou
    own,
  Whose life is not lighted by grace on its way;
For they are true Irish, O yes! they alone,
  Whose hearts are all true on St. Patrick's
    Day.

51.

To Saint Wilfrid.

1 HAIL, holy Wilfrid, hail!
  Kindest of patrons, hail!
  Whose loving help doth ne'er
  Thy trusting children fail!

2 Saint of the cheerful heart,
  Quick step, and beaming eye!
  Give light unto our lives,
  And at our death be nigh!

3 To Mary's lovers thou,
  Sweet Saint! hast shown the road;
  O teach us how to love
  The Mother of our God!

4 Teach us, dear Saint! to make
  The Church our only home;
  To love the faith, the rites,
  And all the ways of Rome!

5 Lover of youth! do thou
  Our English children bless;
  Their joyous hearts' first love
  For Mary's service press.

6 Into our souls, dear Saint!
  With thy blithe courage come,
  And make us missioners
  Of Mary and of Rome!

7 Hail, holy Wilfrid, hail!
  Saint of the free and gay!
  Look how we follow thee,
  And bless us in our way!

52.

My Father.

1 O God! Thy power is wonderful,
    Thy glory passing bright;
  Thy wisdom, with its deep on deep,
    A rapture to the sight.

2 Thy justice is the gladdest thing
    Creation can behold;
  Thy tenderness so meek, it wins
    The guilty to be bold.

3 Yet more than all, and ever more,
    Should we Thy creatures bless,
  Most worshipful of attributes,
    Thine awful holiness.

4 There's not a craving in the mind
    Thou dost not meet and still;
  There's not a wish the heart can have
    Which thou dost not fulfil.

5 I see Thee in the eternal years
    In glory all alone,
  Ere round Thine uncreated fires
    Created light had shone.

6 I see Thee walk in Eden's shade,
    I see Thee all through time;
  Thy patience and compassion seem
    New attributes sublime.

7 I see Thee when the doom is o'er,
　　And outworn time is done,
　Still, still incomprehensible,
　　O God! yet not alone.

8 Angelic spirits, countless souls,
　　Of Thee have drunk their fill;
　And to eternity will drink
　　Thy joy and glory still.

9 Mary, herself a sea of grace,
　　Hath all been drawn from Thine;
　And Thou couldst fill a thousand more
　　From out those depths divine.

10 From Thee were drawn those worlds of life,
　　The Saviour's Heart and Soul;
　And undiminished still Thy waves
　　Of calmest glory roll.

11 All things that have been, all that are,
　　All things that can be dreamed,
　All possible creations, made,
　　Kept faithful, or redeemed;—

12 All these may draw upon Thy power,
　　Thy mercy may command;
　And still outflows Thy silent sea,
　　Immutable and grand.

13 O little heart of mine! shall pain
　　Or sorrow make thee moan,
　When all this God is all for thee,
　　A Father all thine own?

53.

School Hymn.

1 O Jesus! God and Man!
　　For love of children once a child!
　O Jesus! God and Man!
　　We hail Thee Saviour sweet and mild!

2 O Jesus! God and Man!
　　Make us poor children dear to Thee,
　And lead us to Thyself,
　　To love Thee for eternity.

3 O Mary! Mother-Maid!
　　God made thee Mother of the poor!
　Mary! to thee we look,
　　To make our souls' salvation sure.

4 O Mary! Mother dear!
　　Thank God, for us, for all His love;
　And pray that in our faith
　　We all may true and steadfast prove.

5 O Jesus! Mary's Son!
　　On Thee for grace we children call;
　Make us all men to love,
　　But to love Thee beyond them all.

6 O Jesus! bless our work,
　　Our sorrows soothe, our sins forgive;
　O happy, happy they
　　Who in the Church of Jesus live!

7 O God, most great and good,
　　At work or play, by night or day,
　Make us remember Thee,
　　Who dost remember us alway!

54.

The True Shepherd.

FOR THE SCHOOL.

1 I was wandering and weary,
　　When my Saviour came unto me;
　For the ways of sin grew dreary,
　　And the world had ceased to woo me:
　And I thought I heard Him say,
　As He came along His way,
　　O silly Souls come near Me;
　　My sheep should never fear Me;
　　I am the Shepherd true!

2 At first I would not hearken,
　　And put off till the morrow;
　But life began to darken,
　　And I was sick with sorrow;

    And I thought I heard Him say,
    As He came along His way,
       O silly Souls come near Me;
       My sheep should never fear Me;
       I am the Shepherd true!

3 At last I stopped to listen,
    His voice could not deceive me;
  I saw His kind Eyes glisten,
    So anxious to relieve me:
  And I thought I heard Him say,
  As He came along His way,
      O silly Souls come near Me;
      My sheep should never fear Me;
      I am the Shepherd true!

4 He took me on His Shoulder,
    And tenderly He kissed me;
  He bade my love be bolder,
    And said how He had missed me;
  And I'm sure I heard Him say,
  As he went along His way,
      O silly Souls come near Me;
      My sheep should never fear Me;
      I am the Shepherd true!

5 Strange gladness seemed to move Him,
    Whenever I did better;
  And He coaxed me so to love Him,
    As if he was my debtor;
  And I always heard Him say,
  As He went along His way,
      O silly Souls come near Me;
      My sheep should never fear Me;
      I am the Shepherd true!

6 I thought His love would weaken,
    As more and more He knew me;
  But it burneth like a beacon,
    And its light and heat go through me;
  And I ever hear Him say,
  As He goes along His way,
      O silly Souls come near Me;
      My sheep should never fear Me;
      I am the Shepherd true!

7 Let us do then, dearest Brothers'
   What will best and longest please us;
Follow not the ways of others,
   But trust ourselves to Jesus:
We shall ever hear Him say,
As He goes along His way,
     O silly Souls come near Me;
     My sheep should never fear Me;
     I am the Shepherd true!

55.

Faith of our Fathers.

1 FAITH of our Fathers! living still,
   In spite of dungeon, fire, and sword:
Oh, how our hearts beat high with joy
   Whene'er we hear that glorious word:
Faith of our Fathers! Holy Faith!
We will be true to thee till death!

2 Our Fathers, chained in prisons dark,
   Were still in heart and conscience free:
How sweet would be their children's fate,
   If they, like them, could die for thee!
     Faith of our Fathers, &c.

3 Faith of our Fathers! Mary's prayers
   Shall win our country back to thee;
And through the truth that comes from God,
   England shall then indeed be free.
     Faith of our Fathers, &c.

4 Faith of our Fathers! we will love
   Both friend and foe in all our strife:
And preach thee too, as love knows how,
   By kindly words and virtuous life.
     Faith of our Fathers, &c.

56.

Faith of our Fathers.
FOR IRELAND.

1 FAITH of our Fathers! living still,
   In spite of dungeon, fire, and sword:

Oh! Ireland's hearts beat high with joy
  Whene'er they hear that glorious word.
Faith of our Fathers! Holy Faith!
We will be true to thee till death!

2 Our Fathers, chained in prisons dark,
  Were still in heart and conscience free:
How sweet would be their children's fate,
  If they, like them, could die for thee!
    Faith of our Fathers, &c.

3 Faith of our Fathers! Mary's prayers
  Shall keep our country fast to thee;
And through the truth that comes from God,
  O we shall prosper and be free!
    Faith of our Fathers, &c.

4 Faith of our Fathers! we must love
  Both friend and foe in all our strife;
And preach thee too, as love knows how,
  By kindly words and virtuous life.
    Faith of our Fathers, &c.

5 Faith of our Fathers! guile and force
  To do thee bitter wrong unite;
But Erin's Saints shall fight for us,
  And keep undimmed thy blessed light.
    Faith of our Fathers, &c.

6 Faith of our Fathers! distant shores
  Their happy faith to Ireland owe;
Then in our home O shall we not
  Break the dark plots against thee now?
    Faith of our Fathers, &c.

7 Faith of our Fathers! days of old
  Within our hearts speak gallantly:
For ages thou hast stood by us,
  Dear Faith! and now we'll stand by thee.
    Faith of our Fathers, &c.

57.
The Right must win.

1 O it is hard to work for God,
  To rise and take His part
Upon this battle-field of earth,
  And not sometimes lose heart!

2 He hides Himself so wondrously,
　　As though there were no God;
　He is least seen when all the powers
　　Of ill are most abroad:

3 Or He deserts us at the hour
　　The fight is all but lost;
　And seems to leave us to ourselves
　　Just when we need him most.

4 Ill masters good; good seems to change
　　To ill with greatest ease;
　And, worst of all, the good with good
　　Is at cross purposes.

5 The Church, the Sacraments, the Faith,
　　Their up-hill journey take;
　Lose here what there they gain, and, if
　　We lean upon them, break.

6 It is not so, but so it looks;
　　And we lose courage then;
　And doubts will come if God hath kept
　　His promises to men.

7 Ah! God is other than we think;
　　His ways are far above,
　Far beyond reason's height, and reached
　　Only by child-like love.

8 And right is right, since God is God;
　　And right the day must win:
　To doubt would be disloyalty,
　　To falter would be sin!

58.

The Eternal Years.

1 How shalt thou bear the Cross, that now
　　So dread a weight appears?
　Keep quietly to God, and think
　　Upon the Eternal Years.

2 Austerity is little help,
　　Although it somewhat cheers;
　Thine oil of gladness is the thought
　　Of the Eternal Years.

3 Set hours and written rule are good,
    Long prayer can lay our fears;
  But it is better calm for thee
    To count the Eternal Years.

4 Rites are as balm unto the eyes,
    God's word unto the ears;
  But he will have thee rather brood
    Upon the Eternal Years.

5 O! many things are good for souls
    In proper times and spheres;
  Thy present good is in the thought
    Of the Eternal Years.

6 Thy self-upbraiding is a snare,
    Though meekness it appears;
  More humbling is it far for thee
    To face the Eternal Years.

7 Brave quiet is the thing for thee,
    Chiding thy scrupulous fears;
  Learn to be real, from the thought
    Of the Eternal Years.

8 Bear gently, suffer like a child,
    Nor be ashamed of tears;
  Kiss the sweet Cross, and in thy heart
    Sing of the Eternal Years.

9 Thy Cross is quite enough for thee,
    Though little it appears;
  For there is hid in it the weight
    Of the Eternal Years.

10 And know'st thou not how bitterness
    An ailing spirit cheers?
  Thy medicine is the strengthening thought
    Of the Eternal Years.

11 One Cross can sanctify a soul;
    Late saints and ancient seers
  Were what they were, because they mused
    Upon the Eternal Years.

12 Pass not from flower to pretty flower;
 Time flies, and judgment nears;
Go, make thy honey from the thought
 Of the Eternal Years.

13 Death will have rainbows round it, seen
 Through calm contrition's tears,
If tranquil hope but trims her lamp
 At the Eternal Years.

14 Keep unconstrain'dly in this thought
 Thy loves, hopes, smiles, and tears;
Such prison-house thine heart will make
 Free of the Eternal Years.

15 A single practice long sustained
 A soul to God endears:
This must be thine—to weigh the thought
 Of the Eternal Years.

16 He practises all virtue well,
 Who his own Cross reveres,
And lives in the familiar thought
 Of those Eternal Years.

59.

The Sinner invited to the Mission.

1 O COME to the merciful Saviour that calls you,
 O come to the Lord who forgives and forgets;
Though dark be the fortune on earth that befals you,
 There's a bright home above where the sun never sets.

2 O come then to Jesus, whose arms are extended
 To fold His dear children in closest embrace!
O come, for your exile will shortly be ended
 And Jesus will show you his beautiful face!

3 O sons of St. Patrick! dear children of Erin!
 'Tis God that hath kept you your wonderful faith!

Ah, love Him then, love Him; for the dark
  night is nearing,
And the light of His love shall be with you
  in death.

4 Then come to the Saviour, whose mercy grows
    brighter
  The longer you look at the depth of His love;
And fear not! 'tis Jesus! and life's cares grow
    lighter
  As you think of the home and the glory
    above.

5 Have you sinned as none else in the world
    have before you?
  Are you blacker than all other creatures in
    guilt?
O fear not! O fear not! the mother that bore
    you
  Loves you less than the Saviour whose blood
    you have spilt!

6 O come, then, to Jesus, and say how you love
    Him,
  And swear at His feet you will keep in His
    grace;
For one tear that is shed by a sinner can
    move Him,
  And your sins will drop off in His tender
    embrace.

7 Then come to His feet, and lay open your
    story
  Of suffering and sorrow, of guilt and of shame;
For the pardon of sin is the crown of His glory,
  And the joy of our Lord to be true to His
    name.

8 O come, then, to Jesus, and drink of His
    fountains!
  O come, for who needs not His mercy and
    love?
Believe me, dear children, that Erin's green
    mountains
  Are dull to the bright land that waits you
    above.

60.

The Act of Contrition.

1 My God! who art nothing but mercy and kindness,
  O shut not thine ear to the penitent's prayer;
  'Tis Thy grace that hath cured me, dear Lord, of my blindness,
  Thy love that hath lifted me up from despair.

2 O cruel! O cruel! the bondage of evil
  That hath kept me so fast, and held me so low!
  O fearful the hold, the stronghold of the devil,
  And the keen bitter fires of the long hopeless woe!

3 But, O God! by Thy mercy my mind is enlightened;
  I feel a new purpose burn strong in my heart;
  I come to Thee now like a child scared and frightened,
  And I cling to Thy love and will never depart.

4 There is not one evil that sin hath not brought me,
  There is not one good that hath come in its train;
  It hath cursed me through life, and its sorrows have sought me,
  Each day that went by, in want, sickness, or pain.

And O, when this life of affliction was ended,
  What a home for my weary heart did it prepare!
The anger of Him whom my sins had offended,
  And the night, the sick night of eternal despair!

6 Yes! death would have come, and its angel
    have torn me
  By force to the judgment where hope could
    not be;
  And a still darker spirit from thence would
    have borne me
    To unspeakable woes in his wide burning
      sea.

7 Where the worms and the wails and the lashes
    cease never,
    O there my poor soul would have sickened
      of fire,
  And I should be tortured for ever and ever,
    But the pains of eternity never would tire.

8 The corn-field all trampled to mud by the
    cattle,
    The house whose scorched walls have been
      blackened by fire,
  Ah! such was my soul when the desolate battle
    Of sin raged within it, and sinful desire.

9 But away, mortal sin! by the help of my God,
    From thy false poisoned fruits I will firmly
      refrain;
  I have vowed, mortal sin! I have manfully
    vowed,
    I will touch thee not, taste thee not, never
      again.

10 I abjure the dark spirit who fondles yet hates
    me,
    I abjure mortal sin, the black gift he hath
      given;
  I hate it for fear of the fire that awaits me,
    I hate it for hope of God's beautiful heaven.

11 I hate it because the dear Lord that would
    ease us
    Sweated blood when He thought of the
      horror of sin;
  I hate it because it hath crucified Jesus,
    Who hath done all He can the worst
      sinners to win.

12 And I swear to Thee—yes, dearest Jesus!
   O let me,
    In the strength of Thy grace, swear an oath
    unto Thee,
   No sin! never more! if thou wilt not forget
   me,
    But in Thy sweet mercy have mercy on me!

61.

Forgiveness of Injuries.

1 O DO you hear that voice from heaven,—
Forgive, and you shall be forgiven?
No angel hath a voice like this;
Not even Mary's song of bliss
From off her throne can waft to earth
A promise of such priceless worth.

2 Again the music comes from heaven,—
Forgive, and you shall be forgiven.
Softly on every wind that blows
Through the wide earth the promise goes,
Absolving sin and opening heaven,
For we forgive and are forgiven!

3 Yes, we, dear Lord! Thy voice can tell;
That gentle voice, we know it well;
Yet never was it sweet and clear
As now when we this promise hear,—
Poor souls! who sadly doubt of heaven,
Forgive, and you shall be forgiven.

4 Sweet Faith! and can this pledge be true?
And is the duty hard to do?
No one, dear Lord! hath done to me
Such wrong as I have done to Thee!
Why should not all men go to heaven?
They who forgive will be forgiven!

5 Thine offers, earth! to this are dull:
Full mercy to the merciful!
O joy to every soul that lives!
Such beautiful bright words He gives,
Whose royal promise cheapens heaven,—
Forgive, and you shall be forgiven.

6 Then listen to us, Jesus, Lord!
See how we take Thee at Thy word:
O, as we hope with Thee to live,
So from our hearts do we forgive;
And from this hour we do not know
The thought, the thing men mean by foe!

7 Yes! saved and saints we all will be!
All of us, Lord! will come to Thee!
Dear heaven! the work for thee is done,—
How easily, how sweetly won!
Yes! thou art ours, eternal heaven!
For we forgave, and are forgiven.

62.

The Wages of Sin.

1 O what are the wages of sin,
  The end of the race we have run?
We have slaved for the master we chose,
  And what is the prize we have won?

2 We gave away all things for him,
  And O it was much that was given,—
The love of the angels and saints,
  And the chance of our getting to heaven

3 We gave away Jesus and God,
  We gave away Mary and grace,
Prayer and Confession and Mass;
  And now we have finished the race!

4 We are worn out and weary with sin;
  Its pleasures are poor at the best;
From what we remember, not worth
  Half an hour of a conscience at rest.

5 For sin in the hand is not like
  The bright thing it looked to the eye;
Its taste is still worse than its touch;
  Yet we swallow the poison and die.

6 O fools that we were! can we now
  Break off the bad bargains we made?
And is there a way to get back
  The precious deposit we paid?

7 O yes! we have got but to send
    One word or one sigh up to heaven;
  The mischief will all be undone,
    And the past be completely forgiven.

8 Jesus is just what He was,
    On the Cross, as we left Him before,
  All gentleness, mercy, and love,
    Nay, His love and His mercy look more.

9 We will back with our hearts in our hands—
    For the heart is His regular fee:
  Forgive us, dear Jesus, forgive—
    All we want is forgiveness and Thee

63.

Distractions in Prayer.

1 Ah! dearest Lord! I cannot pray,
    My fancy is not free;
  Unmannerly distractions come,
    And force my thoughts from Thee.

2 I cannot pray; yet, Lord! Thou know'st
    The pain it is to me
  To have my vainly struggling thoughts
    Thus torn away from Thee.

3 Ah! Jesus! teach me how to prize
    These tedious hours when I,
  Foolish and mute before thy face,
    In helpless worship lie.

4 Had I kept stricter watch each hour
    O'er tongue, and eye, and ear,
  Had I but mortified all day
    Each joy as it came near,

5 Had I, dear Lord! no pleasure found
    But in the thought of Thee,
  Prayer would have come unsought, and been
    A truer liberty.

6 Yet Thou art oft most present, Lord!
  In weak distracted prayer;
  A sinner out of heart with self
  Most often finds Thee there.

7 And prayer that humbles sets the soul
  From all illusions free,
  And teaches it how utterly,
  Dear Lord! it hangs on Thee.

64.

The Work of Grace.

1 How the light of Heaven is stealing,
  Gently o'er the trembling soul;
  And the shades of bitter feeling
  From the lightened spirit roll.
    Sweetly stealing, sweetly stealing,
    See how grace its way is feeling.*

2 Fairer than the pearly morning
    Comes the softly struggling ray;
  Ah, it is the very dawning
    That precedes eternal day.
      Sweetly stealing, &c.

3 See the tears, the blessed trouble,
    Doubts and fears, and hopes and smiles!
  How the guilt of sin seems double,
    And how plain are Satan's wiles!
      Sweetly stealing, &c.

4 Now the light is growing brighter,
    Fear of hell, and hate of sin;
  Another flash! the heart is lighter;
    Love of God hath entered in.
      Sweetly stealing, &c.

5 Now upon the favourite passion
    Falls a steady ray of grace;

* For singing, "See how grace its way doth feel."

  And the lights of world and fashion
   In the new light fade apace.
    Sweetly stealing, &c.

6 What was sweet hath now grown bitter,
   What was bitter passing sweet ;
  Even penance now seems fitter
   Than the poor world's idle treat.
    Sweetly stealing, &c.

7 See! more light! the spirit tingles
   With contrition's piercing dart,—
  More,—and love divinely mingles
   Ease and gladness with the smart.
    Sweetly stealing, &c.

8 Free! free! the joyous light of heaven
   Comes with full and fair release—
  O God, what light! all sin forgiven,
   Jesus, Mary, love, and peace.
    Sweetly stealing, &c.

65.

A good Confession.

1 The chains that have bound me are flung to the wind,
  By the mercy of God the poor slave is set free ;
 And the strong grace of heaven breathes fresh o'er the mind,
  Like the bright winds of summer that gladden the sea.

2 There was nought in God's world half so dark or so vile
  As the sin and the bondage that fettered my soul ;
 There was nought half so base as the malice and guile
  Of my own sordid passions, or Satan's control.

3 For years I have borne about hell in my breast,
    When I thought of my God it was nothing but gloom;
  Day brought me no pleasure, night gave me no rest,
    There was still the grim shadow of horrible doom.

4 It seemed as if nothing less likely could be
    Than that light should break in on a dungeon so deep;
  To create a new world was less hard than to free
    The slave from his bondage, the soul from its sleep.

5 But the word had gone forth, and said, Let there be light,
    And it flashed through my soul like a sharp passing smart;
  One look to my Saviour, and all the dark night,
    Like a dream scarce remembered was gone from my heart.

6 I cried out for mercy, and fell on my knees,
    And confessed, while my heart with keen sorrow was wrung;
  'Twas the labour of minutes, and years of disease
    Fell as fast from my soul as the words from my tongue.

7 And now—blest be God and the sweet Lord who died!
    No deer on the mountain, no bird in the sky,
  No bright wave that leaps on the dark bounding tide,
    Is a creature so free or so happy as I.

8 All hail, then, all hail, to the dear Precious Blood
    That hath worked these sweet wonders of mercy in me;

May each day countless numbers throng down
  to its flood,
    And God have His glory, and sinners go free.

66.

The Remembrance of Mercy.

1 Why art thou sorrowful, servant of God?
  And what is this dulness that hangs o'er
    thee now?
  Sing the praises of Jesus, and sing them aloud,
    And the song shall dispel the dark cloud
      from thy brow.

2 O is there a thought in the wide world so sweet
  As that God has so cared for us, bad as we
    are,
  That He thinks of us, plans for us, stoops to
    entreat,
    And follows us, wander we ever so far?

3 Then how can the heart e'er be drooping or sad
    That God hath once touched with the light
      of His grace?
  Can the child have a doubt who but lately
    hath laid
    Himself to repose in his father's embrace?

4 And is it not wonderful, servant of God!
    That He should have honoured us so with
      His love,
  That the sorrows of life should but shorten
    the road
    That leads to Himself and the mansion
      above?

5 O then when the spirit of darkness comes down
    With clouds and uncertainties into thy heart,
  One look to thy Saviour, one thought of thy
    crown,
    And the tempest is over, the shadows depart.

6 That God hath once whispered a word in thine ear,
    Or sent thee from heaven one sorrow for sin,
Is enough for a life both to banish all fear,
    And to turn into peace all the troubles within.

7 The schoolmen can teach thee far less about heaven,
    Of the height of God's power, or the depth of His love,
Than the fire in thy heart when thy sin was forgiven,
    Or the light that one mercy brings down from above.

8 Then why dost thou weep? For see! how time flies,
    The time that for loving and praising was given—
Away with thee, child, then, and hide thy red eyes
    In the lap, the kind lap, of thy Father in heaven.

67.

The Pilgrims of the Night.

1 HARK! hark! my soul! angelic songs are swelling
    O'er earth's green fields and ocean's wave-beat shore!
How sweet the truth those blessed strains are telling
    Of that new life when sin shall be no more!
        Angels of Jesus!
        Angels of light!
        Singing to welcome
        The pilgrims of the night.

2 Darker than night life's shadows fall around us,
    And, like benighted men, we miss our mark;

God hides Himself, and grace hath scarcely found us,
　Ere death finds out his victims in the dark
　　Angels of Jesus! &c.

3 Onward we go, for still we hear them singing,
　Come, weary souls! for Jesus bids you come!
And through the dark, its echoes sweetly ringing,
　The music of the Gospel leads us home.
　　Angels of Jesus! &c.

4 Far, far away, like bells at evening pealing,
　The voice of Jesus sounds o'er land and sea,
And laden souls, by thousands meekly stealing,
　Kind Shepherd! turn their weary steps to Thee.
　　Angels of Jesus! &c.

5 Rest comes at length; though life be long and dreary,
　The day must dawn, and darksome night be past;
All journeys end in welcomes to the weary,
　And heaven, the heart's true home, will come at last.
　　Angels of Jesus! &c.

6 Cheer up, my soul! faith's moonbeams softly glisten
　Upon the breast of life's most troubled sea;
And it will cheer thy drooping heart to listen
　To those brave songs which angels mean for thee.
　　Angels of Jesus! &c.

7 Angels! sing on, your faithful watches keeping,
　Sing us sweet fragments of the songs above;
While we toil on, and soothe ourselves with weeping,
　Till life's long night shall break in endless love.
　　　Angels of Jesus!
　　　Angels of light!
　　　Singing to welcome
　　　　The darkness of the night.

68.

The Christian's Song on his March to Heaven.

1 BLEST is the Faith, divine and strong,
　Of thanks and praise an endless fountain,
Whose life is one perpetual song,
　High up the Saviour's holy mountain.
　　O Sion's songs are sweet to sing
　　　With melodies of gladness laden;
　　Hark! how the harps of angels ring,
　　　Hail, Son of Man! Hail, Mother-Maiden!

2 Blest is the hope that holds to God
　In doubt and darkness still unshaken,
And sings along the heavenly road
　Sweetest when most it seems forsaken.
　　O Sion's songs, &c.

3 Blest is the love that cannot love
　Aught that earth gives of best and brightest;
Whose raptures thrill, like saints' above,
　Most when its earthly gifts are lightest.
　　O Sion's songs, &c.

4 Blest is the penance that believes
　That charity turns hell to heaven;
Counts its dark sins, and while it grieves
　Hopes for all that to be forgiven.
　　O Sion's songs, &c.

5 Blest is the time that in the eye
　Of God its hopeful watch is keeping,
And grows into eternity
　Like noiseless trees when men are sleeping.
　　O Sion's songs, &c.

6 Blest is the death that good men die,
　Solemn, self-doubting, firm and wary;
Trusting to God its destiny,
　And leaning for its hour on Mary.
　　O Sion's songs, &c.

69.

Fight for Sion.

1 CHRISTIANS! to the war!
    Gather from afar!
        Hark! hark! the word is given;
    Jesus bids us fight
    "For God and the Right,"
        And for Mary, the Queen of Heaven!
    Now first for thee, thou wicked world!
        Puffed up with godless pomp and pageant
    Avenging grace to humble thee
        Can make the weakest arm its agent.
            Christians! to the war!
            Gather from afar!
                Hark! hark! the word is given;
            Jesus bids us fight
            "For God and the Right,"
                And for Mary, the Queen of Heaven

2 And thou, dark fiend, six thousand years
    The Bride of Christ in vain tormenting,
  Shall find our hate and scorn of thee
    Deep as thine own, and unrelenting.
        Christians! to the war, &c.

3 Ah! Self! so oft forgiven, thou
    Canst play no part but that of traitor.
  We spare thy life; but thou must bear
    The felon's brand, the captive's fetter.
        Christians! to the war, &c.

4 But worse than devil, flesh, or world,
    Human respect, like poison creeping,
  Chills and unnerves the hosts of Christ,
    When weary war-worn hearts are sleeping.
        Christians! to the war, &c.

5 Like lions roaring for their prey,
    Armies of foes are round us trooping;
  What then? see! countless angels come
    To heal the hurt, to raise the drooping.
        Christians! to the war, &c.

6 Then bravely, comrades, to the fight,
    With shout and song each other cheering;
Strength not our own from heaven descends,
    The sun breaks out, the clouds are clearing.
        Christians! to the war, &c.

7 On to the gates of Sion, on!
    Break through the foe with fresh endeavour;
We'll hang our colours up in heaven,
    When peace shall be proclaimed for ever.
        Christians! to the war, &c.

70.

An Evening Hymn at the Oratory.

1 SWEET Saviour! bless us ere we go;
    Thy word into our minds instil;
And make our lukewarm hearts to glow
    With lowly love and fervent will.
Through life's long day and death's dark night,
O gentle Jesus! be our light!

2 The day is done, its hours have run;
    And Thou hast taken count of all,—
The scanty triumphs grace hath won,
    The broken vow, the frequent fall.
        Through life's long day, &c.

3 Grant us, dear Lord! from evil ways
    True absolution and release;
And bless us more than in past days
    With purity and inward peace.
        Through life's long day, &c.

4 Do more than pardon; give us joy,
    Sweet fear and sober liberty;
And simple hearts without alloy,
    That only long to be like Thee.
        Through life's long day, &c.

5 Labour is sweet, for Thou hast toiled;
    And care is light, for Thou hast cared:
Ah! never let our works be soiled
    With strife, or by deceit ensnared.
        Through life's long day, &c.

6 For all we love, the poor, the sad,
    The sinful,—unto Thee we call;
O let Thy mercy make us glad:
    Thou art our Jesus and our All!
        Through life's long day, &c.

7 Sweet Saviour! bless us; night is come,
    Mary and Philip near us be;
Good Angels, watch about our home;
    And we are one day nearer Thee!
        Through life's long day, &c.

71.

The Memory of the Dead.

1 O it is sweet to think
    Of those that are departed,
While murmured Aves sink
    To silence tender-hearted;
While tears that have no pain
    Are tranquilly distilling,
And the dead live again
    In hearts that love is filling.

2 Yet not as in the days
    Of earthly ties we love them;
For they are touched with rays
    From light that is above them:
Another sweetness shines
    Around their well-known features;
God with His glory signs
    His dearly ransomed creatures.

3 Ah! they are more our own,
    Since now they are God's only;
And each one that has gone
    Has left our heart less lonely.
He mourns not seasons fled,
    Who now in Him possesses
Treasures of many dead
    In their dear Lord's caresses.

4 Dear dead! they have become
   Like guardian angels to us;
And distant heaven like home,
   Through them begins to woo us,
Love that was earthly wings
   Its flight to holier places;
The dead are sacred things
   That multiply our graces.

5 They whom we loved on earth
   Attract us now to heaven;
Who shared our grief and mirth
   Back to us now are given.
They move with noiseless foot
   Gravely and sweetly round us,
And their soft touch hath cut
   Full many a chain that bound us.

6 O dearest dead! to heaven
   With grudging sighs we gave you,
To Him—be doubts forgiven!
   Who took you there to save you:—
Now get us grace to love
   Your memories yet more kindly;
Pine for our homes above,
   And trust to God more blindly.

72.
Heaven.

1 O WHAT is this splendour that beams on me now,
   This beautiful sunrise that dawns on my soul?
While faint and far off land and sea lie below,
   And under my feet the huge golden clouds roll.

2 To what mighty king doth this city belong,
   With its rich jewelled shrines, and its gardens of flowers;
With its breaths of sweet incense, its measures of song,
   And the light that is gilding its numberless towers?

3 See! forth from the gates, like a bridal array,
    Come the princes of heaven—how bravely they shine!
  'Tis to welcome the stranger, to show me the way,
    And to tell me that all I see round me is mine!

4 There are millions of saints, in their ranks and degrees,
    And each with a beauty and crown of his own;
  And there, far outnumbering the sands of the seas,
    The nine rings of angels encircle the throne.

5 And far in the heart of that glorious light
    The mighty apostles are seated in state,
  With Joseph and John, who in life's mortal night
    Were appointed on Jesus and Mary to wait.

6 And still deeper in, Mary's splendour is seen,
    Her beautiful self and her choice starry crown;
  And all heaven grows bright in the smile of its queen,
    For the glory of Jesus illumines her throne.

7 And O if the exiles of earth could but win
    One sight of the beauty of Jesus above,
  From that hour they would cease to be able to sin,
    And earth would be heaven; for heaven is love.

8 But words may not tell of the Vision of peace,
    With its worshipful seeming, its marvellous fires;
  Where the soul is at large, where its sorrows all cease,
    And the gift has outbidden its boldest desires!

9 No sickness is here, no bleak bitter cold,
    No hunger, debt, prison, or wearyful toil;
  No robbers to rifle our treasures of gold,
    No rust to corrupt, and no canker to spoil.

10 My God! and it was but a short hour ago
    That I lay on a bed of unbearable pains;
  All was cheerless around me, all weeping and woe,
    Now the wailing is changed to angelical strains.

11 Because I served Thee, were life's pleasures all lost?
    Was it gloom, pain, or blood, that won heaven for me?
  Oh, no! one enjoyment alone could life boast,
    And that, dearest Lord! was my service of Thee!

12 I had hardly to give; 'twas enough to receive,
    Only not to impede the sweet grace from above;
  And this first hour in heaven, I can hardly believe
    In so great a reward for so little a love!

73.

Paradise.

1 O PARADISE! O Paradise!
  Who doth not crave for rest?
Who would not seek the happy land,
  Where they that loved are blest.
    Where loyal hearts, and true,
      Stand ever in the light,
      All rapture through and through,
      In God's most holy sight!

2 O Paradise! O Paradise!
  The world is growing old;
Who would not be at rest and free
  Where love is never cold?
    Where loyal hearts, &c.

3 O Paradise! O Paradise!
　　Wherefore doth death delay;
　Bright death, that is the welcome dawn
　　Of our eternal day;
　　　Where loyal hearts, and true,
　　　　Stand ever in the light,
　　　All rapture through and through,
　　　　In God's most holy sight?

4 O Paradise! O Paradise;
　　'Tis weary waiting here;
　I long to be where Jesus is,
　　To feel, to see Him near.
　　　Where loyal hearts, &c.

5 O Paradise! O Paradise!
　　I want to sin no more!
　I want to be as pure on earth
　　As on thy spotless shore.
　　　Where loyal hearts, &c.

6 O Paradise! O Paradise!
　　I greatly long to see
　The special place my dearest Lord
　　Is furnishing for me.
　　　Where loyal hearts, &c.

7 O Paradise! O Paradise!
　　I feel 'twill not be long;
　Patience! I almost think I hear
　　Faint fragments of thy song.
　　　Where loyal hearts, &c.

Part II.

74.

The Three Kings.

1 Who are these that ride so fast o'er the desert's sandy road,
  That have tracked the Red Sea shore, and have swum the rivers broad;
  Whose camel's bells are tinkling through the long and starry night—
  For they ride like men pursued, like the vanquished of a fight?

2 Who are these that ride so fast? They are eastern monarchs three,
  Who have laid aside their crowns, and renounced their high degree;
  The eyes they love, the hearts they prize, the well-known voices kind,
  Their people's tents, their native plains, they've left them all behind.

3 The very least of faith's dim rays beamed on them from afar,
  And that same hour they rose from off their thrones to track the star;
  They cared not for the cruel scorn of those who called them mad;
  Messiah's star was shining, and their royal hearts were glad.

4 No Bibles and no books of God were in that eastern land,
  No Pope, no blessed Pope, had they to guide them with his hand;

No Holy Roman Church was there, with its
clear and strong sunshine;
With its voice of truth, its arm of power, its
sacraments divine.

5 But a speck was in the midnight sky, uncertain, dim, and far,
And their hearts were pure, and heard a voice
proclaim Messiah's star:
And in its golden twinkling they saw more
than common light,
The Mother and the Child they saw in Bethlehem by night!

6 And what were crowns, and what were thrones,
to such a sight as that?
So straight away they left their tents, and
bade not grace to wait;
They hardly stop to slake their thirst at the
desert's limpid springs,
Nor note how fair the landscape is, how sweet
the skylark sings!

7 Whole cities have turned out to meet their
royal cavalcade,
Wise colleges and doctors all their wisdom
have displayed;
And when the star was dim, they knocked at
Herod's royal gate,
And troubled with the news of faith his politic
estate.

8 And they have knelt in Bethlehem! The
Everlasting Child
They saw upon His Mother's lap, earth's
monarch meek and mild;
His little feet, with Mary's leave, they pressed
with loving kiss,—
O what were thrones, O what were crowns, to
such a joy as this!

9 One little sight of Jesus was enough for many
years,
One look at Him, their stay and staff in the
dismal vale of tears:

Their people for that sight of Him they
    gallantly withstood,
They taught His faith, they preached His
    word, and for Him shed their blood.

10 Ah! me, what broad daylight of faith our
    thankless souls receive,
  How much we know of Jesus, and how easy
    to believe:
  'Tis the noonday of His sunshine, of His sun
    that setteth never:
  Faith gives us crowns, and makes us kings,
    and our kingdom is for ever!

11 O glory be to God on high for these Arabian
    kings,
  These miracles of royal faith, with eastern
    offerings:
  For Gaspar and for Melchior and Balthazzar,
    who from far
  Found Mary out and Jesus by the shining
    of a star!

12 Let us ask these martyrs, then, those monarchs of the East,
  Who are sitting now in heaven at their
    Saviour's endless feast,
  To get us faith from Jesus, and hereafter
    faith's bright home,
  And day and night to thank Him for the
    glorious faith of Rome!

75.

St. Philip and the World.

1 THE world is wise, for the world is old;
  Five thousand years their tale have told
  Yet the world is not happy as the world
    might be—
  Why is it? why is it? O answer me!

2 The world is kind if we ask not too much!
   It is sweet to the taste, and smooth to the touch;
   Yet the world is not happy as the world might be—
   Why is it? why is it? O answer me!

3 The world is strong with an awful strength,
   And full of life in its breadth and length;
   Yet the world is not happy as the world might be—
   Why is it? why is it? O answer me!

4 The world is so beautiful, one may fear
   Its borrowed beauty might make it too dear;
   Yet the world is not happy as the world might be—
   Why is it? why is it? O answer me!

5 The world is good in its own poor way;
   There is rest by night and high spirits by day;
   Yet the world is not happy as the world might be—
   Why is it? why is it? O answer me!

6 This very world saw Messiah's birth,
   And Mary was only a daughter of earth;
   Yet the world is not happy as the world might be—
   Why is it? why is it? O answer me!

7 The Cross shines fair, and the church-bell rings,
   And the earth is peopled with holy things;
   Yet the world is not happy as the world might be—
   Why is it? why is it? O answer me!

8 What lackest thou, world! for God made thee of old?
   Why,—thy faith hath gone out, and thy heart grown cold;
   Thou art not as happy as thou mightest be,
   For the want of Christ's simplicity.

9 It is love that thou lackest, thou poor old world!
Who shall make thy blood hot for thee, frozen old world?
Thou art not as happy as thou mightest be,
For the love of dear Jesus is little in thee.

10 God hath sent thee a Saint new heat to impart;
Love is always at high-water mark in his heart;
He will make thee as happy as thou mayest be;
'Tis St. Philip of Rome who is sent to thee.

11 Now, foolish old world! kick not at his rule!
Be content if he sends thy grey hairs back to school.
He will make thee as happy as thou canst be,
For he will bid Mary pray for thee.

12 Poor world! if thou cravest a better day,
Remember—the Saints must have their own way:
I mourn thou art not as thou mightest be—
But the love of God would do all for thee.

13 And Jesus and Mary would set thee free,
Hadst thou ears to hear, and eyes to see,
What good Father Philip has done for me;
For the love of God is the creature's liberty!

76.

The Emigrant's Song.

1 ALAS! o'er Erin's lessening shores
  The flush of day is fading,
And coldly round us ocean roars,
  The exiled heart upbraiding.
It tells of those whose pining love
  Must cross the seas to find us,
And of the dead at peace above
  Whose graves we leave behind us.

2 Ah! we shall meet no green like thine,
   Erin! where we are going;
No waters to our eyes can shine
   Like Shannon proudly flowing;
No sea-bays we can love so well
   As that round Cove extending,
No fragrance like the bog-fire's smell
   In evening's calm ascending.

3 Poor heart! God knows how sore and long
   The fight hath been within it;
The battle lies not with the strong,
   Or our love of home might win it,—
We could not bear from wife's dear eyes
   Each day to miss the shining,
As oft she strove to hush the cries
   Of babes in famine pining.

4 The very joy of all this earth,
   The blessed name of Jesus,
They turned what was our holiest mirth
   To Satan's snare to tease us.
He sent his troops, with food in hand,
   To their false faith to woo us;
To take the blessing from our land,
   And eternally undo us.

5 'Twas hard to watch the wasting child,
   Nor take the bribe thus given;
Ah, me! a father's heart gone wild,
   For earth might barter heaven,—
The men of stone, they watched their hour,
   Darkness and light were striving;
But Jesus tempered hunger's power,
   We conquered and are living.

6 And now into that sunset far
   Across the western waters,
Freedom of faith and plenty's star
   Lead Erin's sons and daughters.
Dear friends at home! whene'er ye grieve,
   Prayer o'er the sea can find us,
And to our native land we leave
   Blessing and love behind us.

Part III.

77.

Veni Creator.

1 Veni, Creator Spiritus,
  Mentes tuorum visita,
  Imple superna gratia
  Quæ tu creasti pectora.

2 Qui diceris Paraclitus,
  Altissimi donum Dei,
  Fons vivus, ignis, charitas,
  Et spiritalis unctio.

3 Tu septiformis munere
  Digitus Paternæ dexteræ,
  Tu rite promissum Patris,
  Sermone ditans guttura.

4 Accende lumen sensibus,
  Infunde amorem cordibus,
  Infirma nostri corporis
  Virtute firmans perpeti.

5 Hostem repellas longius,
  Pacemque dones protinus;
  Ductore sic te prævio
  Vitemus omne noxium.

6 Per te sciamus da Patrem,
  Noscamus atque Filium,
  Teque utriusque Spiritum
  Credamus omni tempore.

7 Deo Patri sit gloria,
Et Filio, qui a mortuis
Surrexit, ac Paraclito,
In sæculorum sæcula.
               Amen.

78.

Te Deum laudamus.

Te Deum laudamus: te Dominum confitemur.

Te æternum Patrem omnis terra veneratur.

Tibi omnes Angeli; tibi cœli, et universæ potestates:

Tibi Cherubim et Seraphim, incessabili voce proclamant:

Sanctus, Sanctus, Sanctus, Dominus Deus Sabaoth:

Pleni sunt cœli et terra, majestatis gloriæ tuæ.

Te gloriosus Apostolorum chorus.

Te Prophetarum laudabilis numerus.

Te Martyrum candidatus laudat exercitus.

Te per orbem terrarum, sancta confitetur Ecclesia.

Patrem immensæ majestatis.

Venerandum tuum verum et unicum Filium.

Sanctum quoque Paraclitum Spiritum.

Tu Rex gloriæ Christe.

Tu Patris sempiternus es Filius.

Tu ad liberandum suscepturus hominem, non horruisti Virginis uterum.

Tu devicto mortis aculeo, aperuisti credentibus regna cœlorum.

Tu ad dexteram Dei sedes: in gloria Patris.

Judex crederis esse venturus.

* Te ergo quæsumus, tuis famulis subveni: quos pretioso sanguine redemisti.

Æterna fac cum Sanctis tuis, in gloria numerari.

Salvum fac populum tuum, Domine: et benedic hæreditati tuæ.

      * Here it is usual to kneel.

Et rege eos, et extolle illos, usque in æternum.
Per singulos dies, benedicimus te.
Et laudamus nomen tuum in sæculum: et in sæculum sæculi.
Dignare, Domine, die isto: sine peccato nos custodire.
Miserere nostri, Domine: miserere nostri.
Fiat misericordia tua, Domine, super nos: quemadmodum speravimus in te.
In te, Domine, speravi; non confundar in æternum.

79.

O Salutaris Hostia.

1 O salutaris Hostia,
   Quæ cœli pandis ostium:
   Bella premunt hostilia,
   Da robur, fer auxilium.

2 Uni Trinoque Domino
   Sit sempiterna gloria,
   Qui vitam sine termino
   Nobis donet in patria.
       Amen.

80.

Tantum ergo Sacramentum.

1 Tantum ergo Sacramentum
   Veneremur cernui:
   Et antiquum documentum
   Novo cedat ritui;
   Præstet fides supplementum
   Sensuum defectui.

2 Genitori, Genitoque
   Laus et jubilatio,
   Salus, honor, virtus quoque
   Sit et benedictio:
   Procedenti ab utroque
   Compar sit laudatio.
       Amen.

81.

Adeste Fideles.

1 ADESTE fideles,
   Læti triumphantes;
   Venite, venite in Bethlehem:
   Natum videte
   Regem angelorum:
   Venite adoremus,
   Venite adoremus,
   Venite adoremus Dominum.

2 Deum de Deo,
   Lumen de lumine,
   Gestant puellæ viscera:
   Deum verum,
   Genitum, non factum:
     Venite adoremus, &c.

3 Cantet nunc Io!
   Chorus angelorum:
   Cantet nunc aula cœlestium,
   Gloria
   In excelsis Deo!
     Venite adoremus, &c.

4 Ergo qui natus
   Die hodierna,
   Jesu tibi sit gloria,
   Patris æterni
   Verbum caro factum!
     Venite adoremus, &c.

82.

Magnificat.

MAGNIFICAT anima mea Dominum.

Et exultavit spiritus meus: in Deo salutari meo.

Quia respexit humilitatem ancillæ suæ: ecce enim ex hoc beatam me dicent omnes generationes.

Quia fecit mihi magna qui potens est: et sanctum nomen ejus.

Et misericordia ejus a progenie in progenies: timentibus eum.

Fecit potentiam in brachio suo: dispersit superbos mente cordis sui.

Deposuit potentes de sede: et exaltavit humiles.

Esurientes implevit bonis: et divites dimisit inanes.

Suscepit Israel puerum suum: recordatus misericordiæ suæ.

Sicut locutus est ad patres nostros: Abraham, et semini ejus in sæcula.

Gloria Patri, &c.

83.

Litany of the Blessed Virgin.

COMMONLY CALLED THE LITANY OF LORETTO.

KYRIE eleison.
Kyrie eleison.
Christe eleison.
Christe eleison.
Kyrie eleison.
Kyrie eleison.
Christe audi nos.
Christe exaudi nos.
Pater de cœlis Deus,
Fili Redemptor mundi Deus,
Spiritus Sancte Deus,
Sancta Trinitas, unus Deus,
Sancta Maria,
Sancta Dei Genitrix,
Sancta Virgo Virginum,
Mater Christi,
Mater divinæ gratiæ,
Mater purissima,
Mater castissima,
Mater inviolata,
Mater intemerata,

Miserere nobis.

Ora pro nobis.

Mater amabilis,
Mater admirabilis,
Mater Creatoris,
Mater Salvatoris,
Virgo prudentissima,
Virgo veneranda,
Virgo prædicanda,
Virgo potens,
Virgo clemens,
Virgo fidelis,
Speculum justitiæ,
Sedes sapientiæ,
Causa nostræ lætitiæ,
Vas spirituale,
Vas honorabile,
Vas insigne devotionis,
Rosa mystica,
Turris Davidica,
Turris eburnea,
Domus aurea,
Fœderis arca,
Janua cœli,
Stella matutina,
Salus infirmorum,
Refugium peccatorum,
Consolatrix afflictorum,
Auxilium Christianorum,
Regina Angelorum,
Regina Patriarcharum,
Regina Prophetarum,
Regina Apostolorum,
Regina Martyrum,
Regina Confessorum,
Regina Virginum,
Regina Sanctorum omnium,
Regina sine labe originali concepta,

Ora pro nobis.

Agnus Dei, qui tollis peccata mundi,
Parce nobis, Domine.
Agnus Dei, qui tollis peccata mundi,
Exaudi nos, Domine.
Agnus Dei, qui tollis peccata mundi,
Miserere nobis.

84.

Salve Regina.

Salve, Regina, mater misericordiæ;
Vita, dulcedo, et spes nostra, salve.
Ad te clamamus, exules filii Hevæ;
Ad te suspiramus, gementes et flentes in hac lacrymarum valle.
Eia ergo, Advocata nostra,
Illos tuos misericordes oculos ad nos converte;
Et Jesum benedictum fructum ventris tui,
Nobis post hoc exilium ostende,
O clemens, O pia, O dulcis Virgo Maria.

85.

Ave Maris Stella.

1 Ave maris stella,
  Dei Mater alma,
  Atque semper virgo,
  Felix cœli porta.

2 Sumens illud Ave
  Gabrielis ore,
  Funda nos in pace,
  Mutans Hevæ nomen.

3 Solve vincla reis,
  Profer lumen cæcis,
  Mala nostra pelle,
  Bona cuncta posce.

4 Monstra te esse matrem,
  Sumat per te preces,
  Qui pro nobis natus,
  Tulit esse tuus.

5 Virgo singularis,
  Inter omnes mitis,
  Nos culpis solutos,
  Mites fac et castos.

6 Vitam præsta puram,
　Iter para tutum,
　Ut videntes Jesum,
　Semper collætemur.

7 Sit laus Deo Patri,
　Summo Christo decus,
　Spiritui Sancto,
　Tribus honor una.
　　　　　　Amen.

86.

From Pain to Pain.

[Verse sung at the Way of the Cross at the Oratory.]

FROM pain to pain, from woe to woe,
With loving hearts and footsteps slow,
To Calvary with Christ we go.
　See how His precious Blood
　　At every station pours;
　Was ever grief like His!
　Was ever sin like ours!

87.

Stabat Mater.

1 STABAT Mater dolorosa
　Juxta crucem lacrymosa,
　　Dum pendebat Filius.
　Cujus animam gementem,
　Contristatam, et dolentem,
　　Pertransivit gladius.

2 O quam tristis et afflicta
　Fuit illa benedicta
　　Mater Unigeniti.
　Quæ mœrebat, et dolebat,
　Pia Mater, dum videbat
　　Nati pœnas inclyti.

3 Quis est homo qui non fleret,
　Matrem Christi si videret
　　In tanto supplicio?

Quis non posset contristari,
  Christi Matrem contemplari
    Dolentem cum Filio?

4 Pro peccatis suæ gentis
  Vidit Jesum in tormentis,
    Et flagellis subditum.
  Vidit suum dulcem Natum
  Moriendo desolatum,
    Dum emisit spiritum.

5 Eia Mater, fons amoris,
  Me sentire vim doloris
    Fac, ut tecum lugeam.
  Fac ut ardeat cor meum
  In amando Christum Deum,
    Ut sibi complaceam.

6 Sancta Mater, istud agas,
  Crucifixi fige plagas
    Cordi meo valide.
  Tui Nati vulnerati,
  Tam dignati pro me pati,
    Pœnas mecum divide.

7 Fac me tecum pie flere,
  Crucifixo condolere,
    Donec ego vixero.
  Juxta Crucem tecum stare,
  Et me tibi sociare
    In planctu desidero.

8 Virgo virginum præclara,
  Mihi jam non sis amara;
    Fac me tecum plangere.
  Fac ut portem Christi mortem,
  Passionis fac consortem,
    Et plagas recolere.

9 Fac me plagis vulnerari,
  Fac me Cruce inebriari,
    Et cruore Filii.
  Flammis ne urar succensus,
  Per te, Virgo, sim defensus
    In die judicii.

10 Christe, cum sit hinc exire,
   Da per Matrem me venire
     Ad palmam victoriæ.
   Quando corpus morietur,
   Fac ut animæ donetur
     Paradisi gloria.
                        Amen.

88.

Miserere.

Miserere mei, Deus: secundum magnam misericordiam tuam.

Et secundum multitudinem miserationum tuarum: dele iniquitatem meam.

Amplius lava me ab iniquitate mea: et a peccato meo munda me.

Quoniam iniquitatem meam ego cognosco: et peccatum meum contra me est semper.

Tibi soli peccavi, et malum coram te feci: ut justificeris in sermonibus tuis, et vincas cum judicaris.

Ecce enim in iniquitatibus conceptus sum: et in peccatis concepit me mater mea.

Ecce enim veritatem dilexisti: incerta et occulta sapientiæ tuæ manifestasti mihi.

Asperges me hyssopo, et mundabor: lavabis me, et super nivem dealbabor.

Auditui meo dabis gaudium et lætitiam: et exultabunt ossa humiliata.

Averte faciem tuam a peccatis meis: et omnes iniquitates meas dele.

Cor mundum crea in me, Deus: et spiritum rectum innova in visceribus meis.

Ne projicias me a facie tua: et Spiritum sanctum tuum ne auferas a me.

Redde mihi lætitiam salutaris tui: et spiritu principali confirma me.

Docebo iniquos vias tuas: et impii ad te convertentur.

Libera me de sanguinibus, Deus Deus salutis meæ: et exultabit lingua mea justitiam tuam.

Domine, labia mea aperies: et os meum annuntiabit laudem tuam.

Quoniam si voluisses sacrificium, dedissem utique: holocaustis non delectaberis.

Sacrificium Deo spiritus contribulatus: cor contritum et humiliatum, Deus, non despicies.

Benigne fac, Domine, in bona voluntate tua Sion: ut ædificentur muri Jerusalem.

Tunc acceptabis sacrificium justitiæ, oblationes, et holocausta: tunc imponent super altare tuum vitulos.

Gloria, &c.

89.

De Profundis.

DE profundis clamavi ad te, Domine: Domine, exaudi vocem meam.

Fiant aures tuæ intendentes: in vocem deprecationis meæ.

Si iniquitates observaveris, Domine: Domine, quis sustinebit?

Quia apud te propitiatio est: et propter legem tuam sustinui te, Domine.

Sustinuit anima mea in verbo ejus: speravit anima mea in Domino.

A custodia matutina usque ad noctem: speret Israel in Domino.

Quia apud Dominum misericordia: et copiosa apud eum redemptio.

Et ipse redimet Israel, ex omnibus iniquitatibus ejus.

Requiem æternam dona eis Domine.

Et lux perpetua luceat eis.

90.

Lent.

1 Now are the days of humblest prayer,
 When consciences to God lie bare,
 And mercy most delights to spare.
    O hearken when we cry,
      Chastise us with Thy fear;
    Yet, Father! in the multitude
      Of Thy compassions, hear!

2 Now is the season, wisely long,
 Of sadder thought and graver song,
 When ailing souls grow well and strong.
    O hearken, &c.

3 The feast of penance! O so bright,
 With true conversion's heavenly light,
 Like sunrise after stormy night.
    O hearken, &c.

4 O happy time of blessed tears,
 Of surer hopes, of chastening fears,
 Undoing all our evil years.
    O hearken, &c.

5 We, who have loved the world, must learn
 Upon that world our backs to turn,
 And with the love of God to burn.
    O hearken, &c.

6 Vile creatures of such little worth,
 Than we, O there are none on earth
 More fallen from their Christian birth.
    O hearken, &c.

7 Full long in sin's dark days we went,
 Yet now our steps are heavenward bent,
 And grace is plentiful in Lent.
    O hearken, &c.

8 All glory to redeeming grace,
 Disdaining not our evil case,
 But showing us our Saviour's face!
    O hearken, &c.

LONDON:
PRINTED BY LEVEY, ROBSON, AND FRANKLYN,
Great New Street and Fetter Lane.

ORATORY TUNES.

LONDON:
BURNS AND LAMBERT,
PORTMAN STREET, PORTMAN SQUARE,
AND 63 PATERNOSTER ROW.

No. 1—THE HOLY TRINITY.

Have mer-cy on us, God most High! Who lift our hearts to Thee; Have mer-cy on us worms of earth, most Ho-ly Tri-ni-ty.

2—THE ETERNAL FATHER.

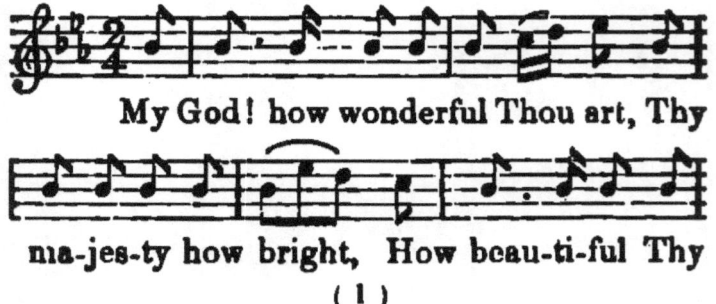

My God! how wonderful Thou art, Thy ma-jes-ty how bright, How beau-ti-ful Thy

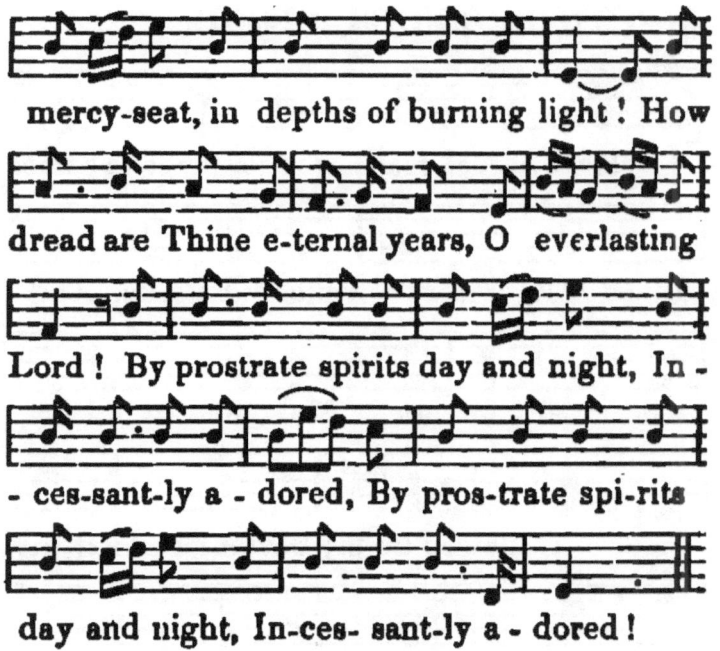

mercy-seat, in depths of burning light! How dread are Thine eternal years, O everlasting Lord! By prostrate spirits day and night, Incessantly adored, By prostrate spirits day and night, Incessantly adored!

3—JESUS CRUCIFIED.

O come and mourn with me awhile; See, Mary calls us to her side! O come and let us mourn with her Jesus our love is crucified.

4—THE PRECIOUS BLOOD.

Hail, Jesus! Hail! who for my sake Sweet Blood from Ma-ry's veins didst take, And shed it all for me, And shed it all for me. O blessed be my Saviour's Blood, my life, my light, my only good, my life, my light, my on-ly good, To all e-ter-ni-ty.

5—ST. PHILIP'S CONVERTS.

Sweet Saint Phi-lip, thou hast won us, Though our hearts were hard as stone; Sin had

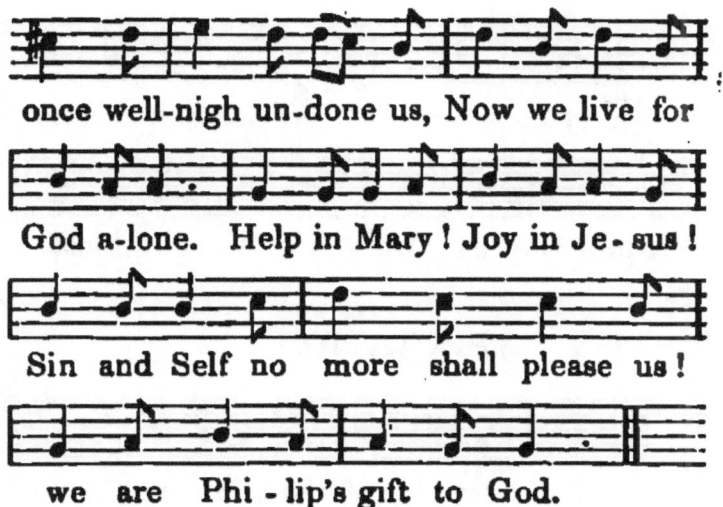

once well-nigh un-done us, Now we live for God a-lone. Help in Mary! Joy in Je-sus! Sin and Self no more shall please us! we are Phi-lip's gift to God.

6—DAILY, DAILY.

Daily! dai-ly sing to Mary, Sing, my soul, her prais-es due; All her feasts, her actions worship, With the heart's de-vo-tion true. Lost in wond'ring contemplation, Be her

Ma-jesty con-fest: Call her Mother, call her  Vir-gin, Hap-py Mo-ther, Vir-gin blest.

7—THE EXPECTATION.

Like the dawning of the morn-ing On the  Mountains' golden heights, Like the breaking  of the moon-beams On the gloom of cloudy  nights; Like a secret told by angels, Get-ting  known upon the earth, Was the Mother's expect--a-tion. Of Messiah's spee-dy birth.

8—THE SOULS IN PURGATORY.

O turn to Je-sus Mother! turn, And

call Him by His tend'rest names;

Pray for the Ho-ly Souls that burn This

hour a-mid the cleans-ing flames.

9—HAIL! HOLY JOSEPH.

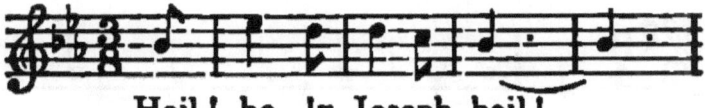
Hail! ho-ly Joseph, hail!

Husband of Ma-ry, hail; chaste as the li-ly

flow'r In Eden's peaceful vale.

10—MOTHER OF MERCY.

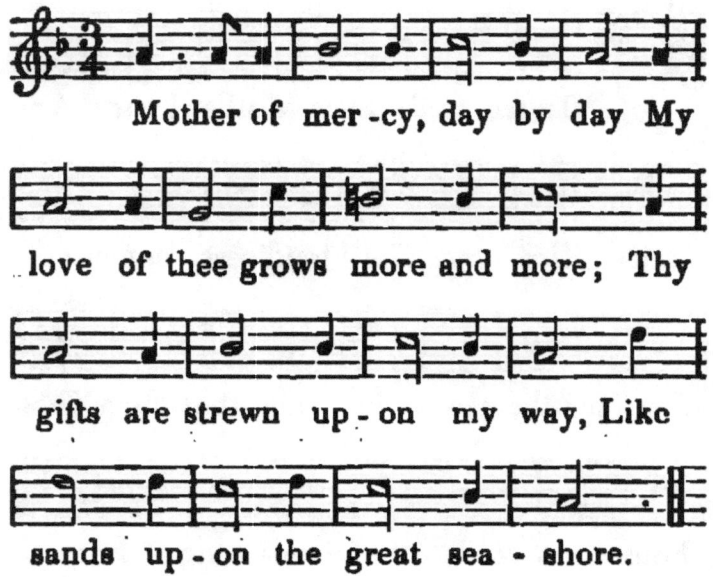

Mother of mer-cy, day by day My love of thee grows more and more; Thy gifts are strewn up-on my way, Like sands up-on the great sea-shore.

11—THE IMMACULATE CONCEPTION.

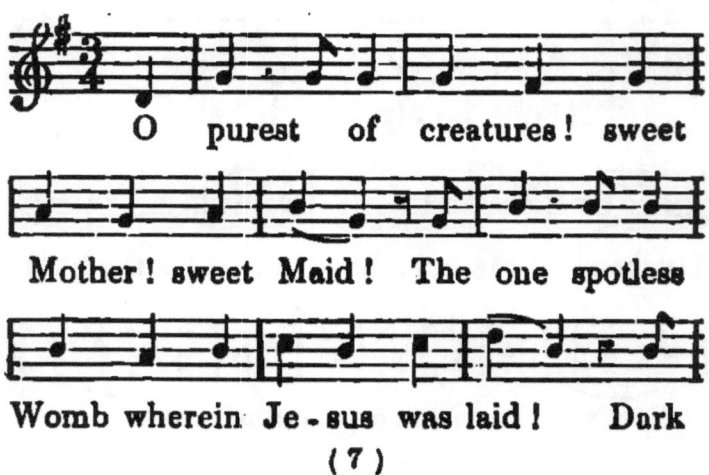

O purest of creatures! sweet Mother! sweet Maid! The one spotless Womb wherein Je-sus was laid! Dark

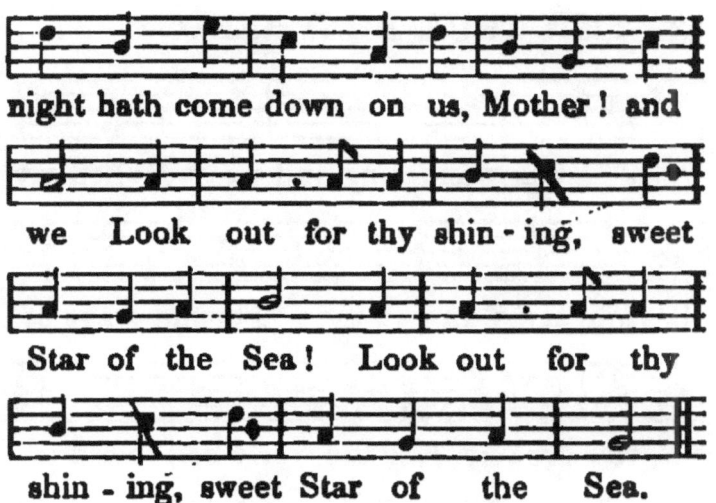

night hath come down on us, Mother! and we Look out for thy shin-ing, sweet Star of the Sea! Look out for thy shin-ing, sweet Star of the Sea.

12—THE DOLOURS OF MARY.

God of mer-cy! let us run Where yon fount of sor-row flows, Pon-d'ring sweet-ly, one by one, Je-su's wounds and Ma-ry's woes.

13—THE TRUE SHEPHERD.

I was wandering and weary, When my Saviour came un-to me; For the ways of sin grew drea-ry, And the world had ceas'd to woo me; And I thought I heard Him say, As He came a-long His way, O sil-ly souls! come near me; My sheep should ne-ver fear Me, My sheep should ne-ver fear Me; I am the Shep-herd true!

14—FAITH OF OUR FATHERS.

Faith of our Fathers! liv-ing still In spite of dun-geon, fire, and sword: Oh! Ire-land's hearts beat high with joy When-e'er they hear that glo-rious word. Faith of our Fa-thers! Ho-ly Faith! We will be true to thee till death! Faith of our Fa-thers! Ho-ly Faith! We will be true to thee till death!

15—THE INFANT JESUS.

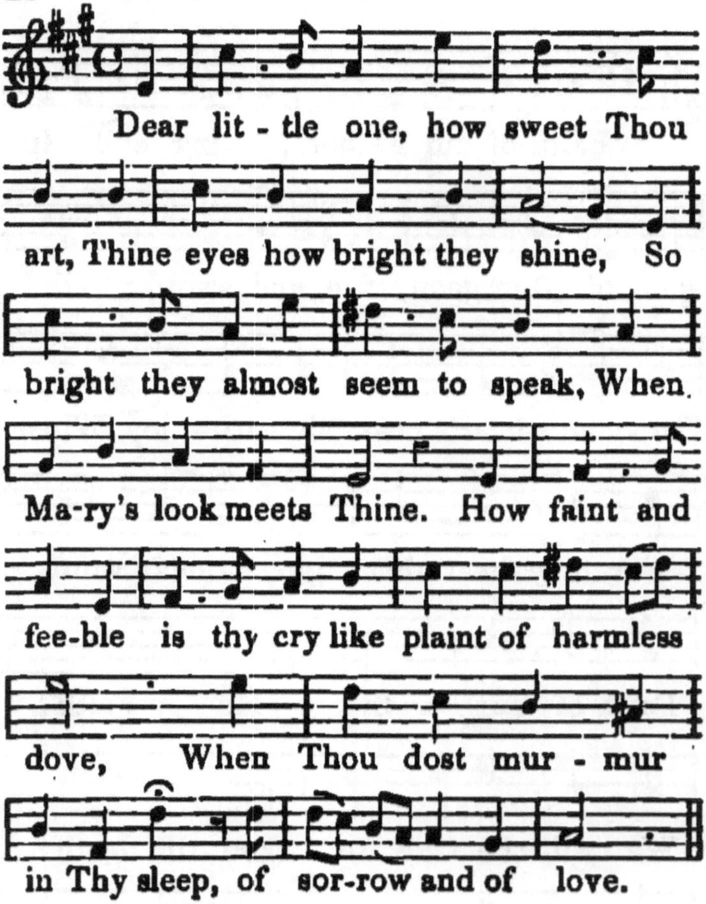

Dear lit-tle one, how sweet Thou art, Thine eyes how bright they shine, So bright they almost seem to speak, When Ma-ry's look meets Thine. How faint and fee-ble is thy cry like plaint of harmless dove, When Thou dost mur-mur in Thy sleep, of sor-row and of love.

16—THE AGONY.

O soul of Je-sus, sick to

(11)

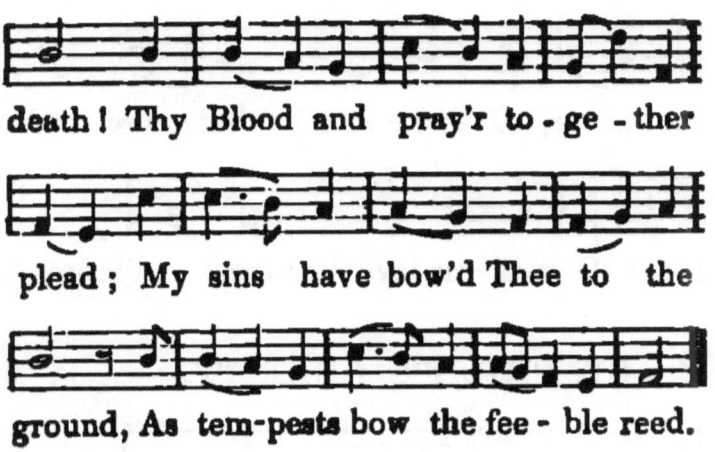

death! Thy Blood and pray'r to-ge-ther plead; My sins have bow'd Thee to the ground, As tem-pests bow the fee-ble reed.

17—THE BLESSED SACRAMENT.

Je-su! my Lord, my God, my all! How can I love thee as I ought? And how revere this wondrous gift so far surpassing hope or thought sweet Sa-cra-ment! we

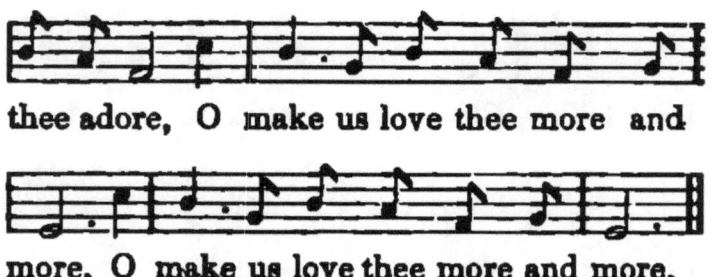

thee adore, O make us love thee more and more, O make us love thee more and more.

18—ST. PHILIP'S CHARITY.

All ye who love the ways of sin, Come to St. Philip's feet and learn The baits that Je-sus hath to win His tru-ant children to re-turn, All praise and thanks to Je-sus be, For sweet St. Phi-lip's cha-ri-

-ty, All praise and thanks to Jesus be, For sweet St. Philip's charity.

19—THE GOOD CONFESSION.

The chains that have bound me are flung to the wind, By the mercy of God the poor slave is set free; And the strong grace of Heaven breathes fresh o'er the mind, Like the bright winds of summer that gladden the sea.

20—THE ASSUMPTION.

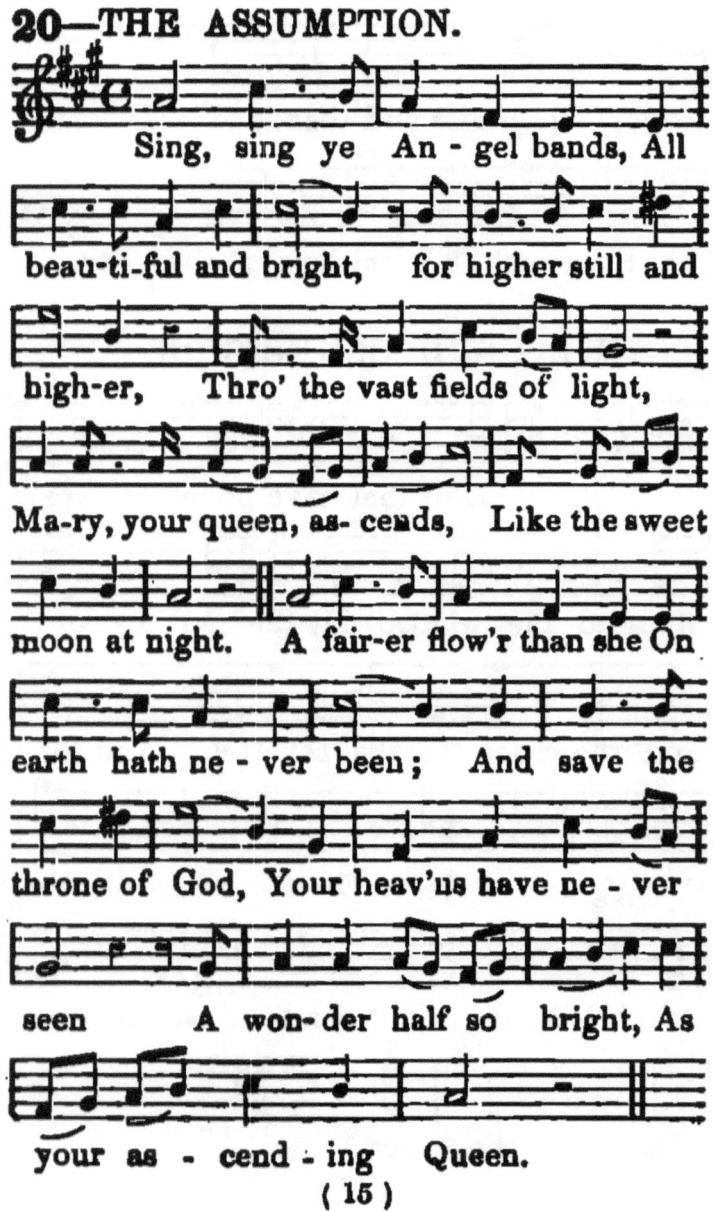

Sing, sing ye Angel bands, All beautiful and bright, for higher still and higher, Thro' the vast fields of light, Mary, your queen, ascends, Like the sweet moon at night. A fairer flow'r than she On earth hath never been; And save the throne of God, Your heav'ns have never seen A wonder half so bright, As your ascending Queen.

21—THE FLOWER OF GRACE.

O Flow'r of grace! divinest Flow'r! God's light thy life, God's love thy dow'r! That all alone with virgin ray Dost make in heaven eternal May, Sweet falls the peerless dignity of God's eternal choice on thee! Mother dearest! Mother fairest! Maiden purest! Maiden rarest! Help of earth and

(16)

joy of heaven! Love and praise to thee be

given, Bliss-ful Mo-ther! Blissful Maiden!

22—THE PENITENT'S PRAYER.

My God, who art nothing but mercy and

kindness, Oh shut not thine ear to the

pe-nitent's praye'r; Tis thy grace that hath

cured me, dear Lord, of my blindness, Thy

love that hath lifted me up from des-pair,

23—O JESUS! DEAREST LORD!

O Jesus, Jesus! dearest Lord! Forgive me if I say, For ve-ry love, Thy sa-cred name A thousand times a-day, A thousand times a-day.

24—VENI, CREATOR.

Come, Ho-ly Ghost, Cre-a-tor come, The darkness of our minds illume; Thy chil-dren's hearts, O God, in-spire, And lighten with ce-les-tial fire.

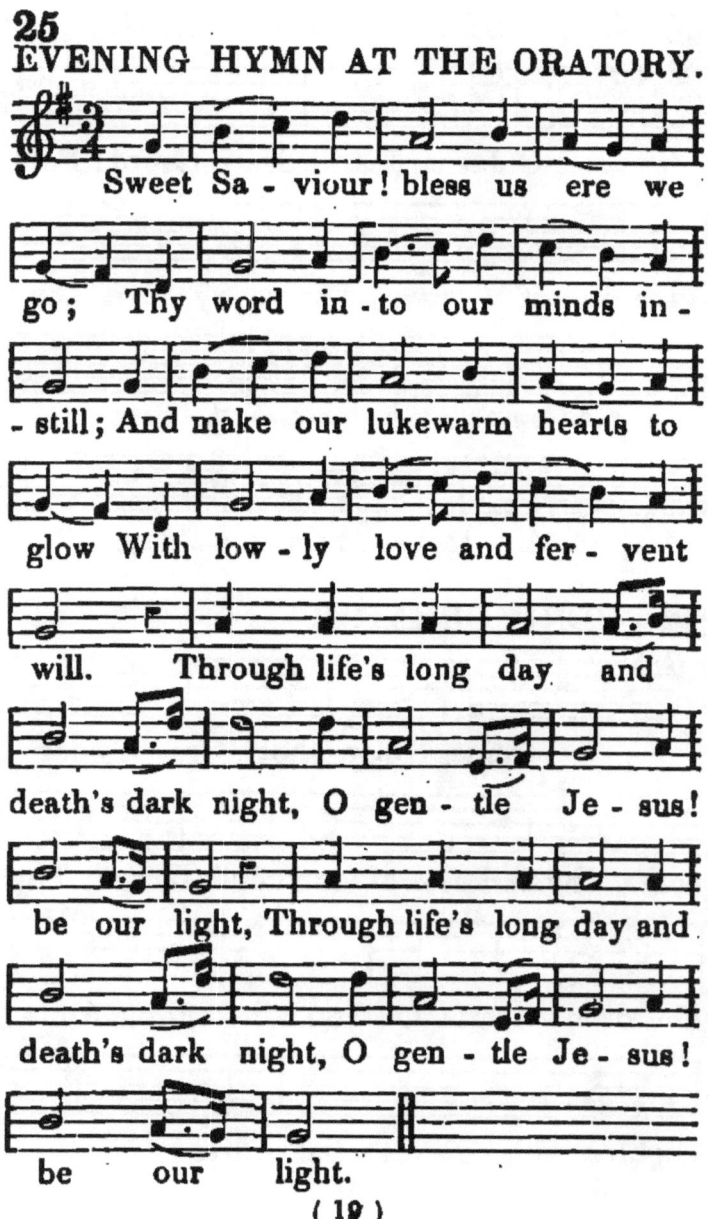

26—PATRONAGE OF ST. JOSEPH.

Dear Hus-band of Ma-ry! dear nurse of her Child! Life's ways are full weary, the desert is wild! Bleak sands are all round us, no home can we see; Sweet Spouse of our Lady! we lean upon Thee.

27—JESUS RISEN.

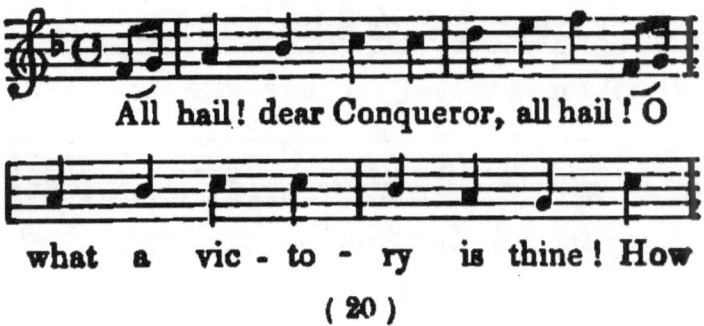

All hail! dear Conqueror, all hail! O what a vic-to-ry is thine! How

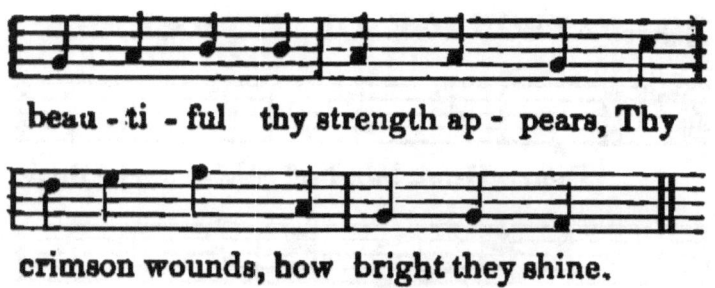

beau - ti - ful thy strength ap - pears, Thy

crimson wounds, how bright they shine.

28—ST. PHILIP'S PICTURE.

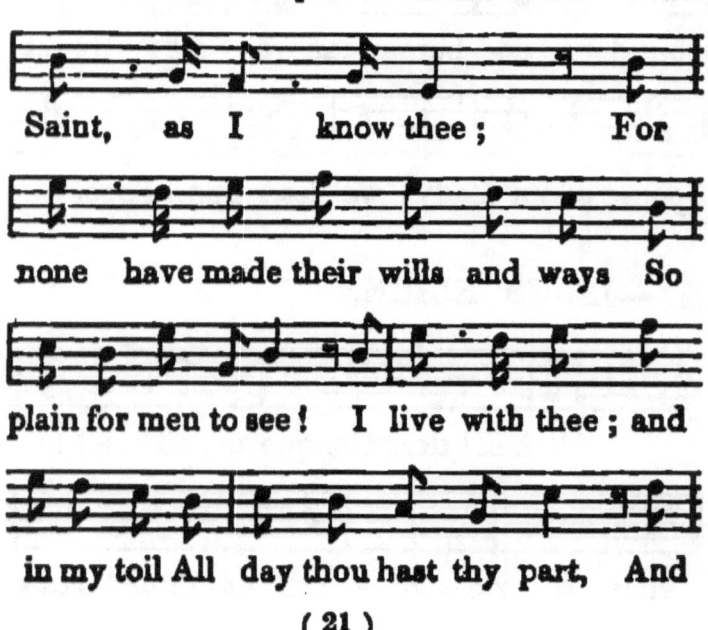

Saint Phi-lip! I have ne- ver known A

Saint, as I know thee; For

none have made their wills and ways So

plain for men to see! I live with thee; and

in my toil All day thou hast thy part, And

then I come at night to learn Thy  pic-ture off by heart.

29—INVITATION TO THE MISSION.

O come to the mer-ci-ful  Sa-viour that calls you, O come to the  Lord who for-gives and for-gets! Tho'  dark be the for-tune on earth that be--falls you, There's a bright home above where the  sun ne-ver sets

30—O HAPPY FLOWERS!

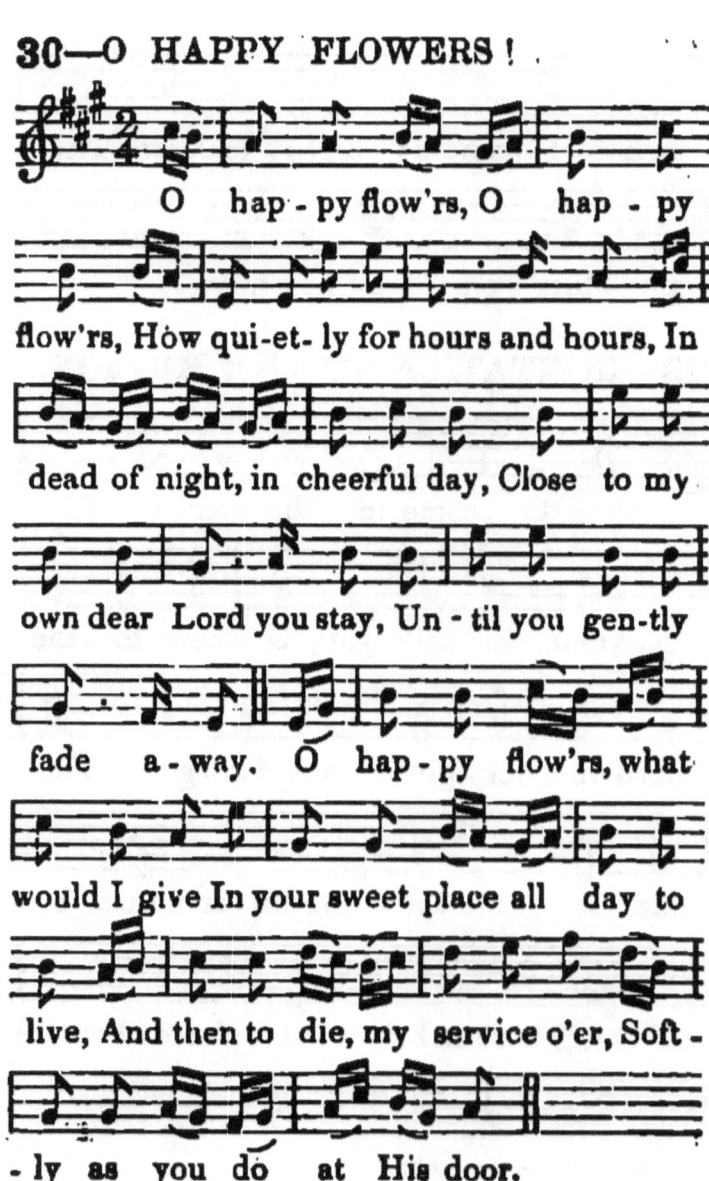

O hap-py flow'rs, O hap-py flow'rs, How qui-et-ly for hours and hours, In dead of night, in cheerful day, Close to my own dear Lord you stay, Un-til you gen-tly fade a-way. O hap-py flow'rs, what would I give In your sweet place all day to live, And then to die, my service o'er, Soft-ly as you do at His door.

31—ST VINCENT DE PAUL.

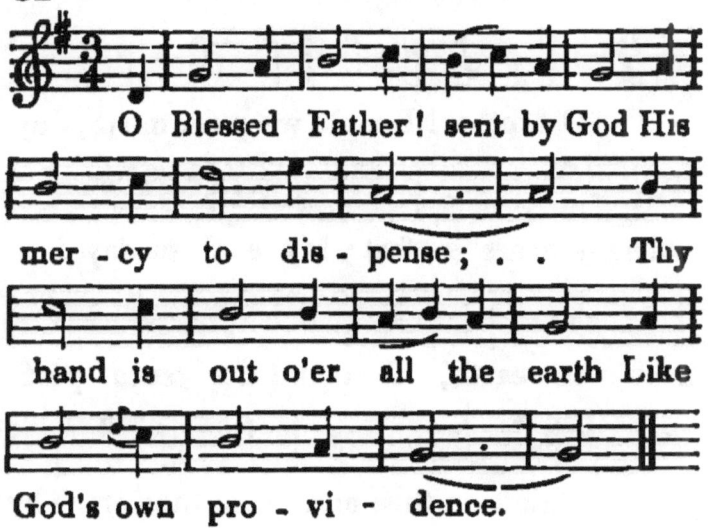

O Blessed Father! sent by God His mer-cy to dis-pense; .. Thy hand is out o'er all the earth Like God's own pro-vi-dence.

32—SCHOOL HYMN.

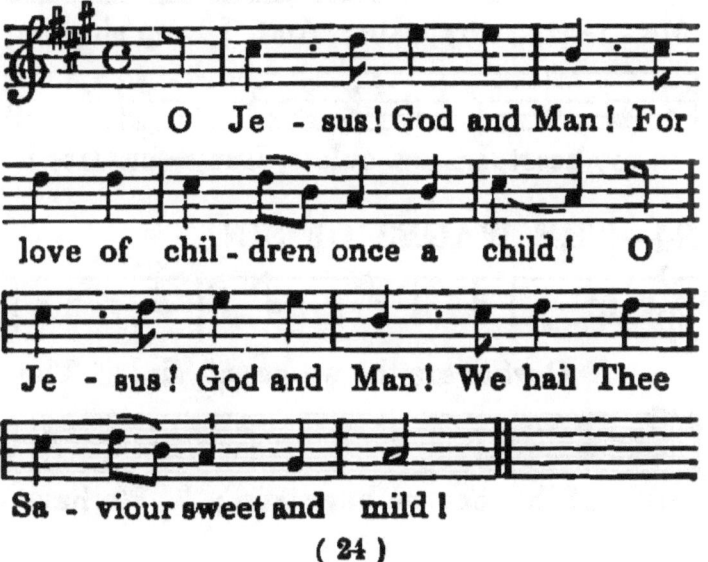

O Je-sus! God and Man! For love of chil-dren once a child! O Je-sus! God and Man! We hail Thee Sa-viour sweet and mild!

33—IMMACULATE, IMMACULATE!

O Mother! I could weep for mirth, Joy fills my heart so fast; My soul to-day is heav'n on earth, O could the trans-port last. I think on thee and what thou art, Thy Ma-jes-ty, thy state; And I keep sing-ing in my heart, Im-ma-culate, Imma-cu-late!

34—THE WAGES OF SIN.

O what are the wa-ges of sin, The end of the race we have run; We have slaved for the Master we chose, And what is the prize we have won?

35—HAIL! HOLY WILFRID, HAIL!

Hail! holy Wilfrid, hail!
Kindest of patrons, hail! Whose loving help doth ne'er Thy trusting children fail!
Saint of the cheerful heart, Quick step and beaming eye! Give light unto our lives, And at our death be nigh.

36—THE FORGIVENESS OF INJURIES.

O dost thou hear the voice from Heav'n, For-give and ye shall be for-given! No An-gel hath a voice like this; Not e-ven Ma-ry's song of bliss, From off her throne can waft to earth A promise of such priceless worth.

37—THE SACRED HEART.

Un-chang-ing and Unchangea-ble, be-fore an-ge-lic eyes, The vi-sion of the

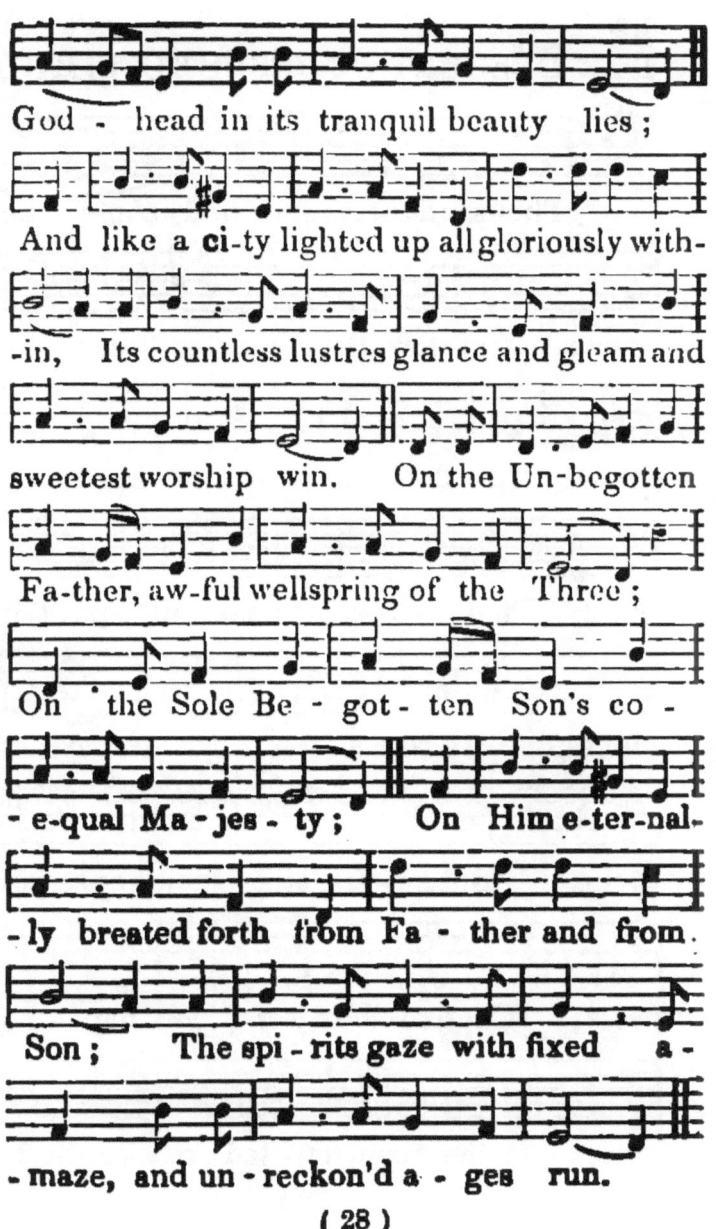
(28)

38
THE DESCENT OF JESUS TO LIMBUS.

Thousands of years had come and gone, And slow the ages seem'd to move To those ex-pec-tant souls, that fill'd That pri-son-house of pa-tient love; It was a wea-ry watch of theirs, But onward still their hopes would press; Captives they were, yet hap-py too, In their con-ten-ted wea-ri-ness.

39—THE GUARDIAN ANGEL.

Dear Angel! e-ver at my side, How loving must thou be, To leave thy home in Heav'n to guard, A guilty wretch like me. Thy beau-ti-ful and shining face I see not, though so near; The sweetness of thy soft low voice I am too deaf to hear.

40—PARADISE.

O Paradise! O Pa-radise! Who would not crave for rest! Who

would not seek that hap-py land, Where they that lov'd are blest. Where loy-al hearts and true, Stand e-ver in the light, All raptured thro' and thro' In God's most ho-ly sight.

41

Oh it is sweet to think Of those that are de-part-ed, While murmur'd a-ves sink To silence tender-hearted; While

43—VENI, SANCTI SPIRITUS.

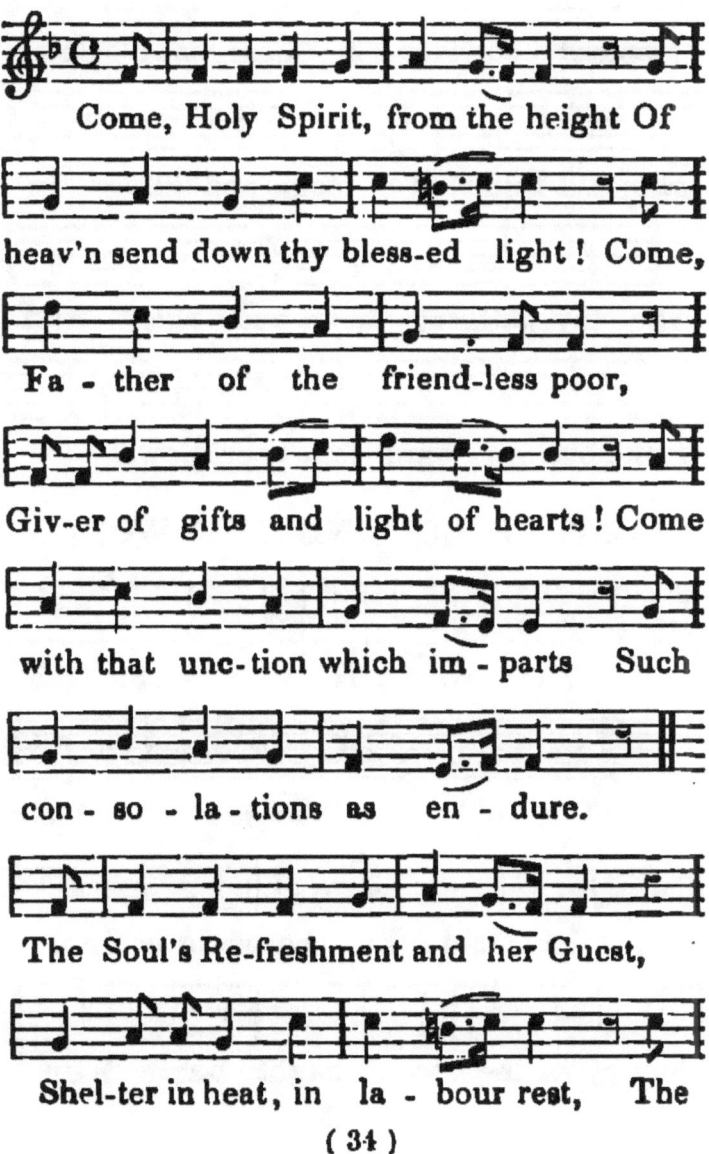

Come, Holy Spirit, from the height Of heav'n send down thy bless-ed light! Come, Fa-ther of the friend-less poor, Giv-er of gifts and light of hearts! Come with that unc-tion which im-parts Such con-so-la-tions as en-dure.

The Soul's Re-freshment and her Guest, Shel-ter in heat, in la-bour rest, The

sweetest so-lace in our woe! Come,
bliss-ful Light! O come and fill, In
all thy faithful, heart and will, And
make our in-ward fer-vour glow.

44—ST. PHILIP AND THE WORLD.

The world is wise, for the
world is old; Five thousand years their
tale have told; Yet the world is not
hap-py as the world might be; Why

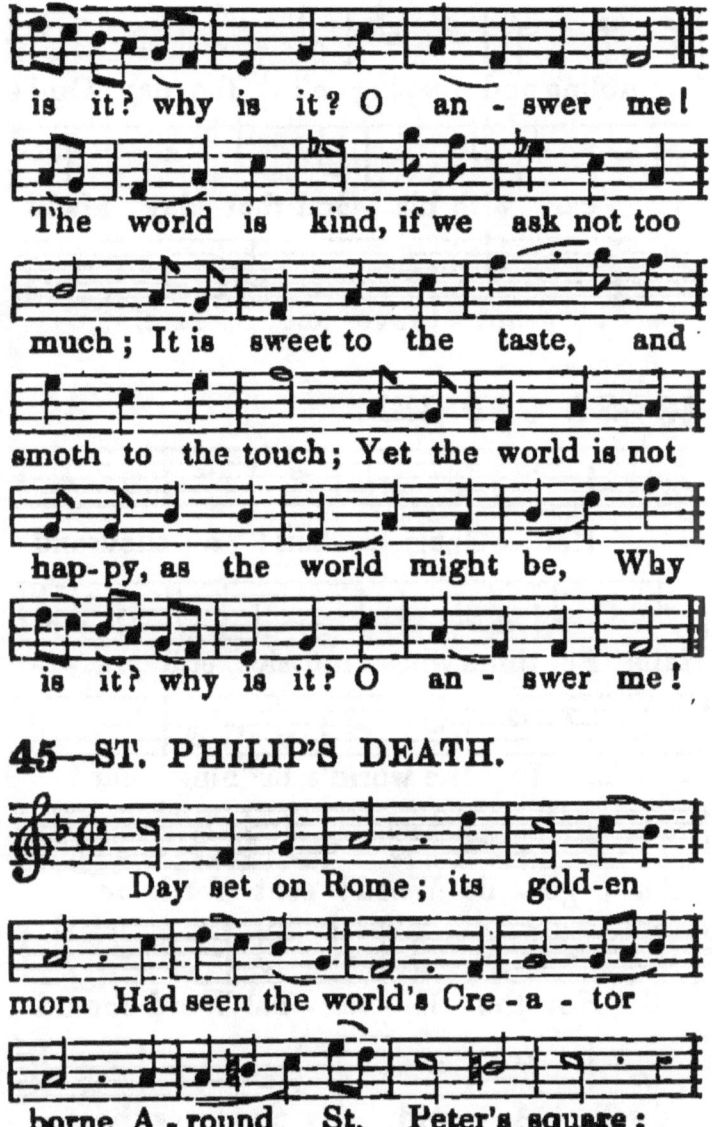

is it? why is it? O an-swer me!

The world is kind, if we ask not too much; It is sweet to the taste, and smoth to the touch; Yet the world is not hap-py, as the world might be, Why is it? why is it? O an-swer me!

45—ST. PHILIP'S DEATH.

Day set on Rome; its gold-en morn Had seen the world's Cre-a-tor borne A-round St. Peter's square;

Trembling and weeping all the day, God's vi-car with his God that day Made pa-geant brave and rare.

46—ST. GABRIEL.

Hail, Gabriel, hail! a thousand Hails For thine whose mu-sic still pre-vails, In the world's list'ning ear! An-ge-lic Word! sent forth to tell How the E-ter-nal Word should dwell A-mid His creatures here.

47—CHRISTMAS DAY.

Ye faith-ful, ap-proach ye, Joyful-ly tri-umphing; Oh come ye, oh come ye to Beth - le-hem; Come and be-hold ye Born the King of An-gels! Oh come, let us worship, oh come, let us wor-ship, oh come, let us wor-ship Christ the Lord! Come and be-hold ye Born the King of Angels! Oh come, let us wor-ship, oh come, let us wor-ship, oh  come, let us wor - ship Christ the Lord!

48—MONTH OF MAY.

Joy of my heart! O let me pay
To Thee thine own sweet month of May. 
Ma-ry, one gift I beg of Thee, 
My soul from sin and sor - row free. 
Direct my wand'ring feet a - right, 
And be thy - self mine own true light.

Be love of Thee the purg-ing fire,
To cleanse for God my heart's de-sire.

49—THE ASCENSION.

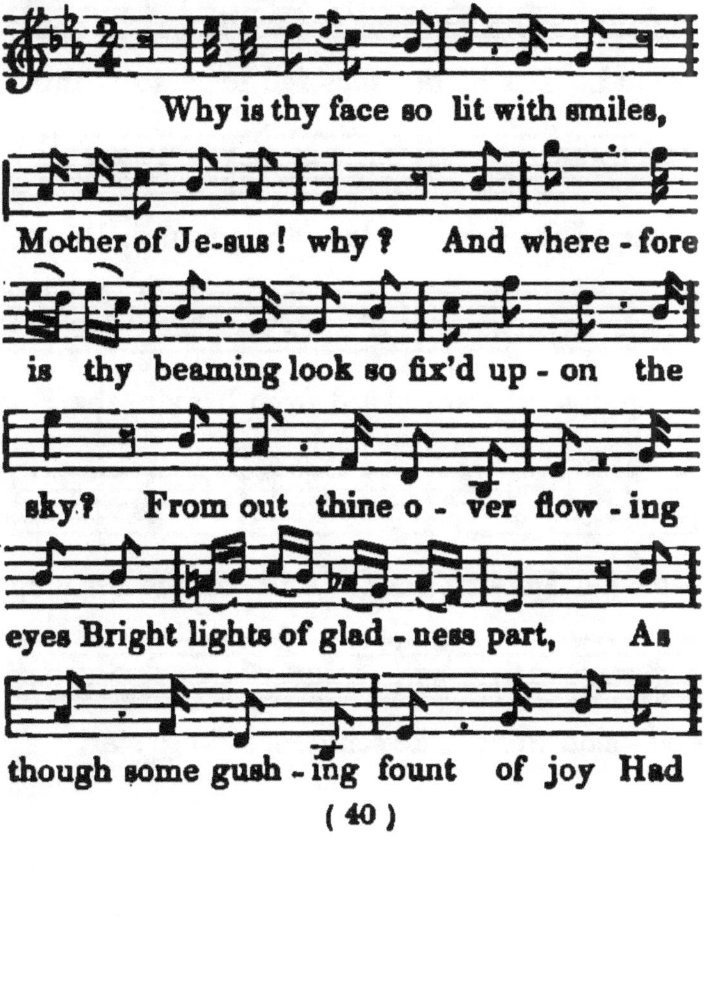

Why is thy face so lit with smiles, Mother of Je-sus! why? And where-fore is thy beaming look so fix'd up-on the sky? From out thine o-ver flow-ing eyes Bright lights of glad-ness part, As though some gush-ing fount of joy Had

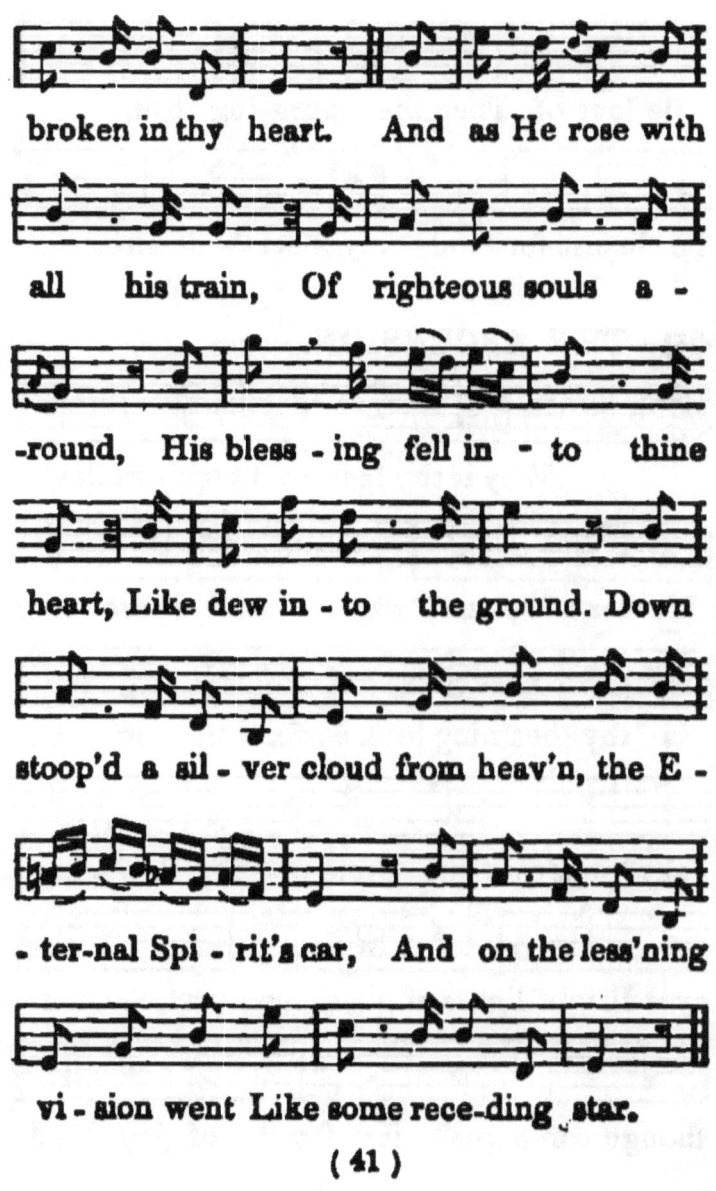

50. ST. PATRICK'S DAY.

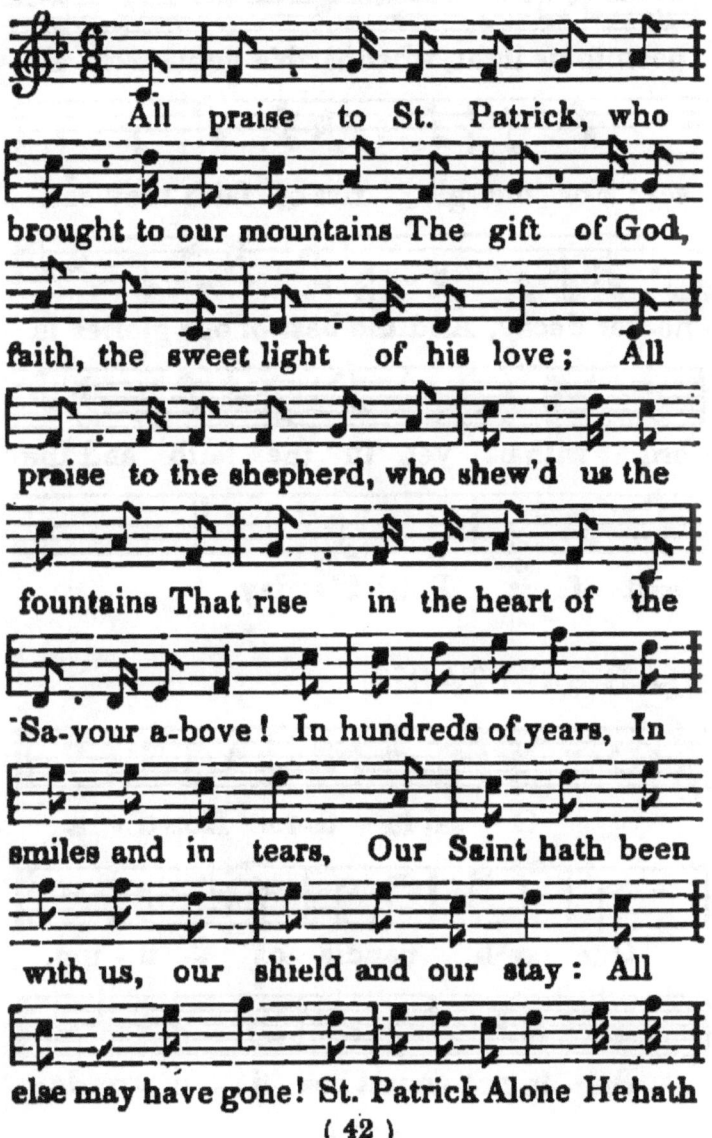

All praise to St. Patrick, who brought to our mountains The gift of God, faith, the sweet light of his love; All praise to the shepherd, who shew'd us the fountains That rise in the heart of the Sa-vour a-bove! In hundreds of years, In smiles and in tears, Our Saint hath been with us, our shield and our stay: All else may have gone! St. Patrick Alone He hath been to us light, when earth's lights were all set; For the glo - ries of faith they can ne-ver decay, And the best of our glories is bright with us yet, In the faith and the feast of St. Patrick's day.

51—O SALUTARIS.

O sa-lu-ta-ris Hos-ti-a.
Qua cœ-li pandis os-ti-um.
Bel-la pre-munt hos-ti-li-a da-

-ro-bur fer au - xi - - li - um. U -
- ni - tri - no - que Do - mi - no. Sit
sem -pi - ter - na glo - ri - a.
Qui vi - tam si - ne ter - mi - no no -
- bis do - net in pa - - tri - a.

52—TANTUM ERGO.

Tantum er - go sa - cra - mentum
ve - ne - re - mur cer - nu - i, Et an - tiquum
documentum, No - vo - ce - dat ri - tu - i,

Præs-tet fi - des sup - ple - men - tum sen - su - um de fec - - tu - i.

53
LITANIES OF OUR BLESSED LADY.

Ky - ri - e e - lei - son. Ky - ri - e e - lei - son. Chris - te e - lei - son, Chris - te e - lei - - son.

Ky - ri - e e - lei - son, Ky - ri - e e - lei - son. Chris - te e - lei - son, Chris - te e - lei - - son.

54—THE PILGRIMS OF THE NIGHT.

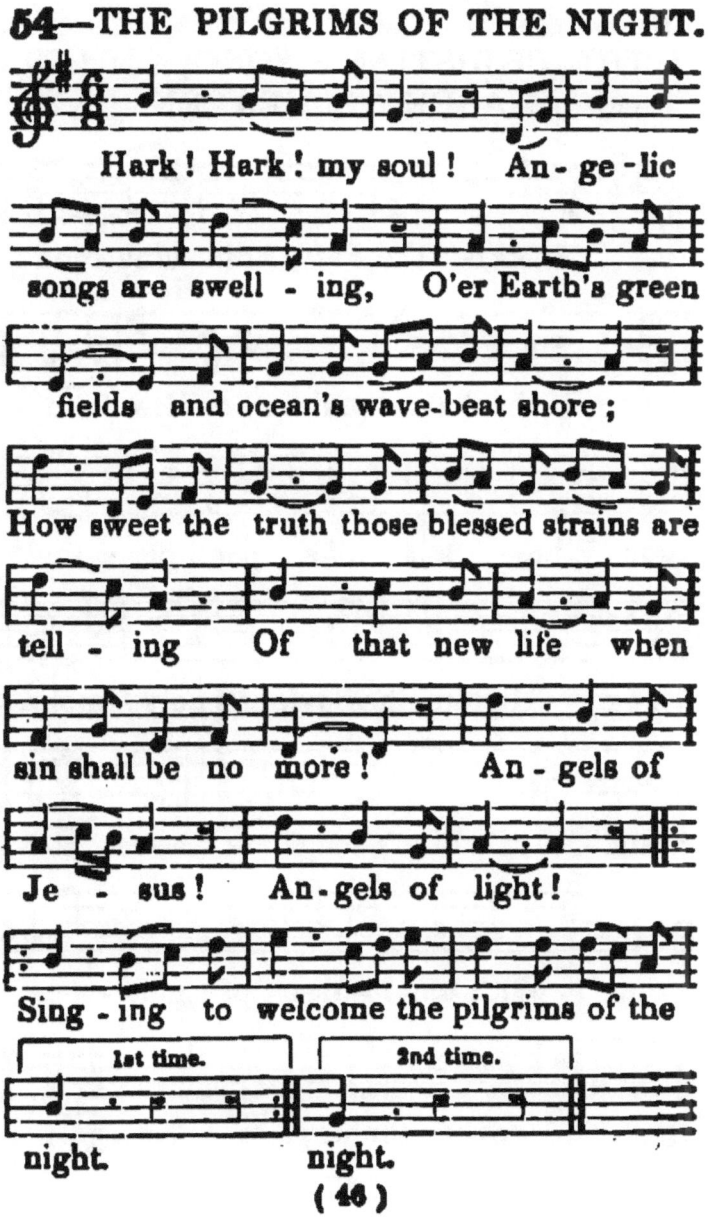

55
THE CHRISTIAN'S SONG, ON HIS MARCH TO HEAVEN.

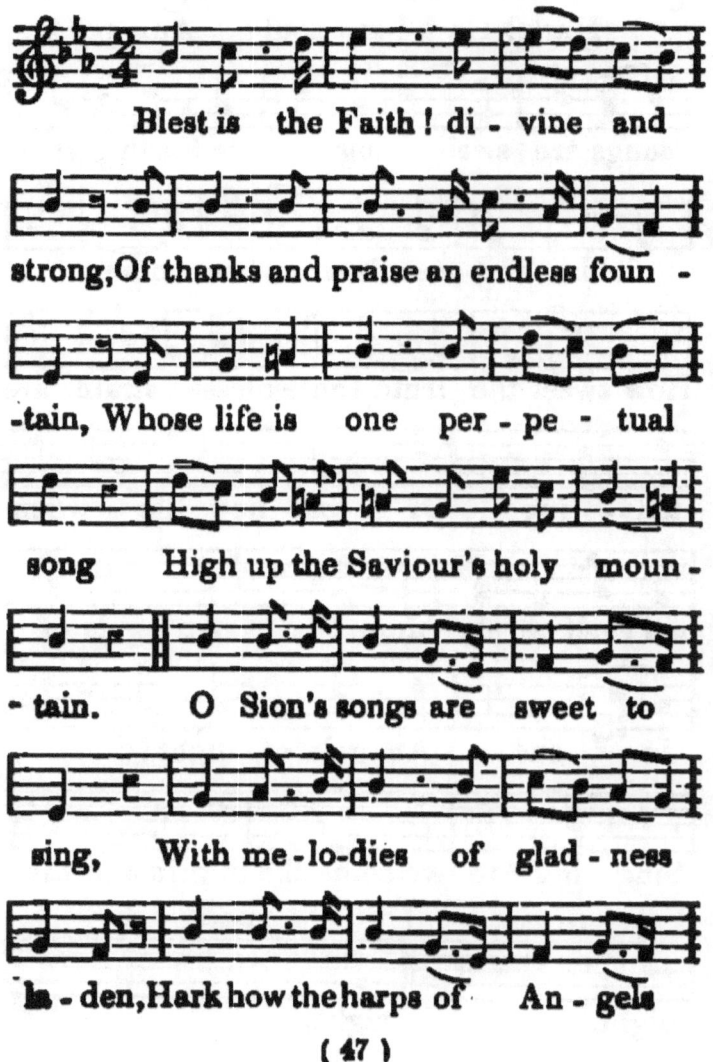

Blest is the Faith! di-vine and strong, Of thanks and praise an endless foun-tain, Whose life is one per-pe-tual song High up the Saviour's holy moun-tain. O Sion's songs are sweet to sing, With me-lo-dies of glad-ness la-den, Hark how the harps of An-gels

-in us good and ho-ly Is from Thee, thy precious gift; In all our joys, in all our sorrows, Wistful hearts to Thee we lift. Holy

58
THANKSGIVING AFTER COMMUNION.

Je-sus, gentlest Saviour! God of might and pow'r! Thou Thy-self art dwelling In us at this hour. Nature can-not hold Thee, Heav'n is all too strait For thine endless glo-ry, And thy roy-al

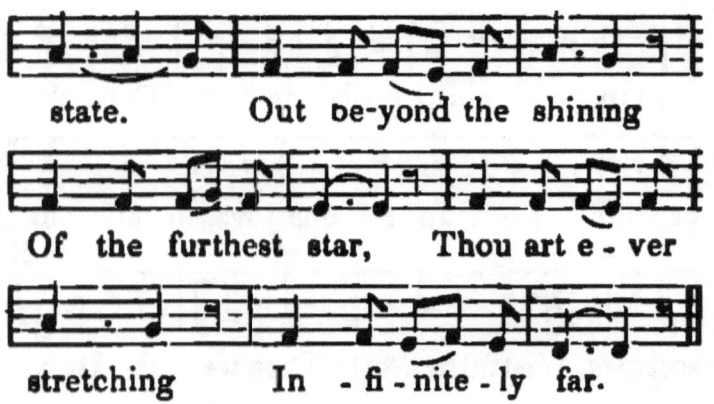

59—THE WORK OF GRACE.

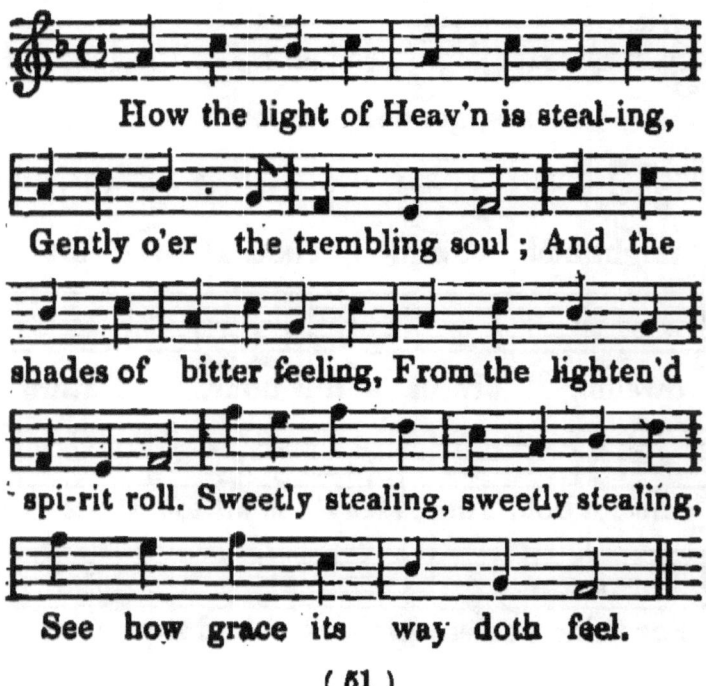

60—THE EMIGRANT'S SONG.

Alas! o'er Erin's less'ning shores The flush of day is fading, And coldly round us ocean roars, The exil'd heart upbraiding. It tells of those whose pining love Must cross the seas to find us; And of the dead at peace above, Whose graves we leave behind us.

61—SWEET MOTHER-MAID.

The moon is in the heavens a-bove, And its light lies on the foamy sea; So shines the star of Mary's love, O'er this stor-my scene of mi-se-ry. Our hands to life's hard work are laid, But our hearts are thine, sweet Mo-ther-Maid.

62—THE RIGHT MUST WIN

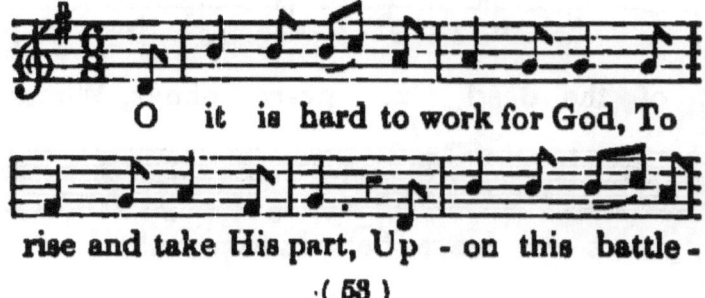

O it is hard to work for God, To rise and take His part, Up-on this battle-

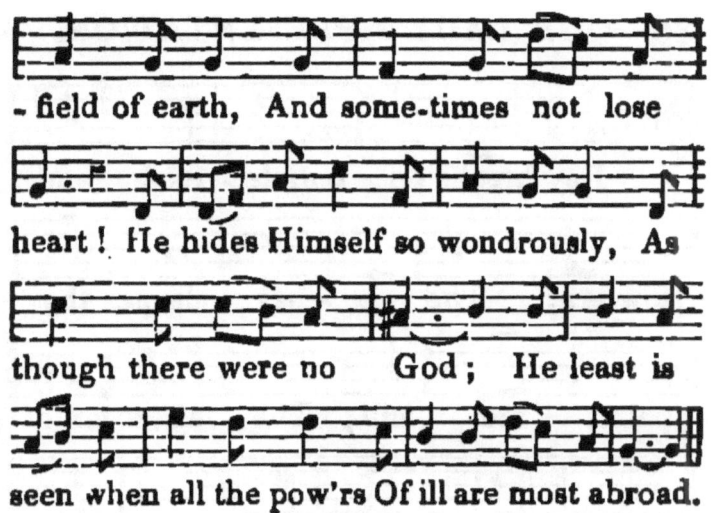

- field of earth, And some-times not lose heart! He hides Himself so wondrously, As though there were no God; He least is seen when all the pow'rs Of ill are most abroad.

63—DISTRACTIONS IN PRAYER.

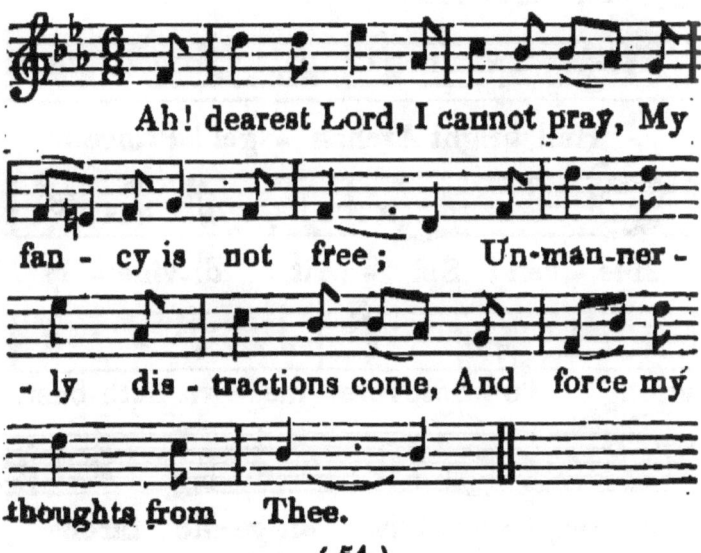

Ah! dearest Lord, I cannot pray, My fan-cy is not free; Un-man-ner-ly dis-tractions come, And force my thoughts from Thee.

64—OUR LADY'S PRESENTATION.

Day breaks on temple-roofs and tow-ers; The ci-ty sleeps, the palms are still; The fairest far of earth's fair flow'rs, Mounts Sion's sacred hill.

65—ST. MICHAEL.

Hail, bright Archan-gel! Prince of Hea-ven! Spi-rit di-vine-ly strong! To whose rare me-rit hath been gi-ven, To head the an-ge-lic throng

66—JESUS IS GOD.

Jesus is God! the solid earth, the o-cean broad and bright, The countless stars like gold-en dust that strew the skies at night, The raging storm, the dreadful fire, the pleasant wholesome air, The sum-mer's sun, the winter's frost, His own cre-a-tion were.

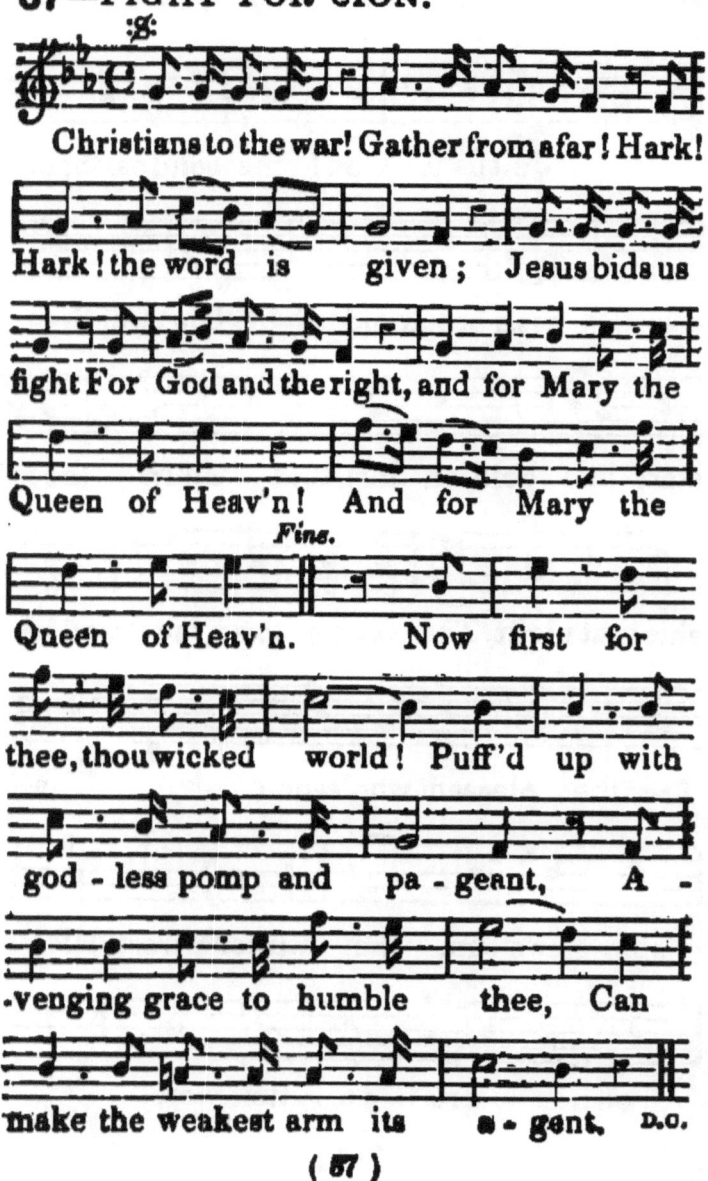

68—THE STATIONS.

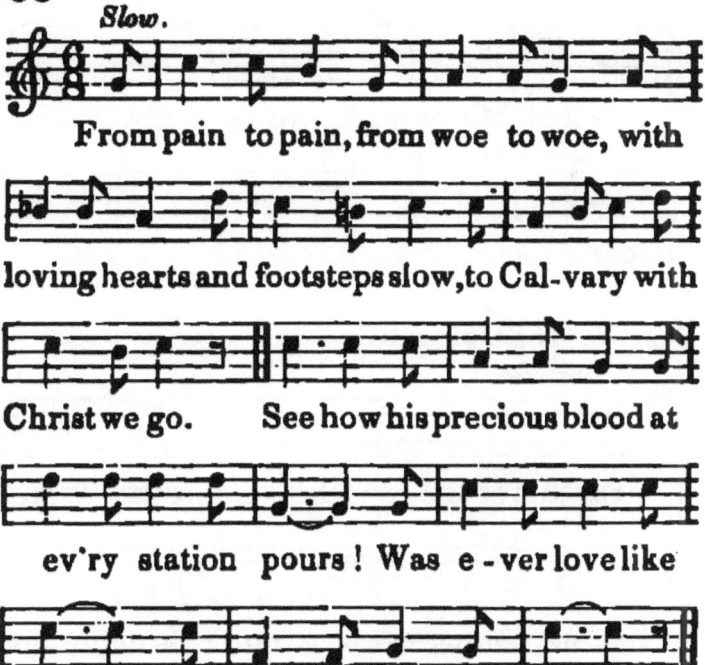

From pain to pain, from woe to woe, with loving hearts and footsteps slow, to Cal-vary with Christ we go. See how his precious blood at ev'ry station pours! Was e-ver love like His, was e-ver sin like ours?

69—STABAT MATER. No. 1.

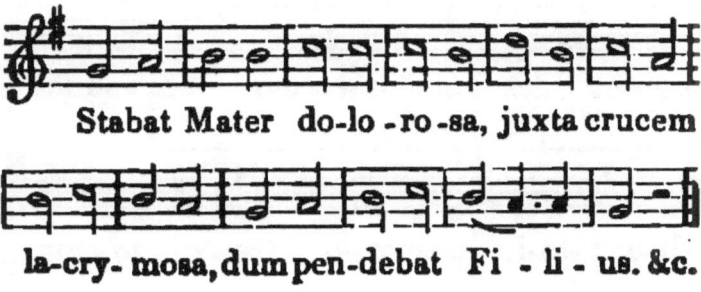

Stabat Mater do-lo-ro-sa, juxta crucem la-cry-mosa, dum pen-debat Fi-li-us. &c.

STABAT MATER No. 2.

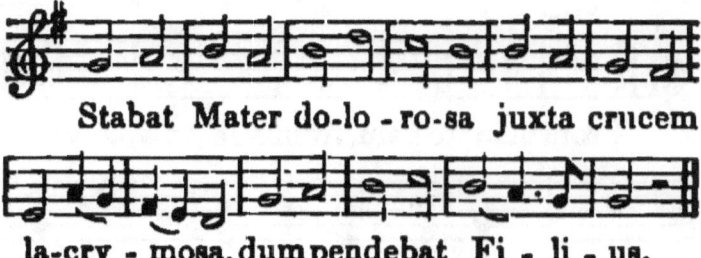

Stabat Mater do-lo-ro-sa juxta crucem la-cry-mosa, dum pendebat Fi-li-us.

70—TANTUM ERGO.

Celebrant.
Tantum er-go Sa-cra-men-tum,
Chorus.
ve-ne-remur cer - - nu-i: et antiquum documentum no-vo ce-dat ri-tu-i; præstet fides supple-mentum sen-suum de-fec-tu-i. *Celebrant.* Genito-ri, Ge-ni-to-que

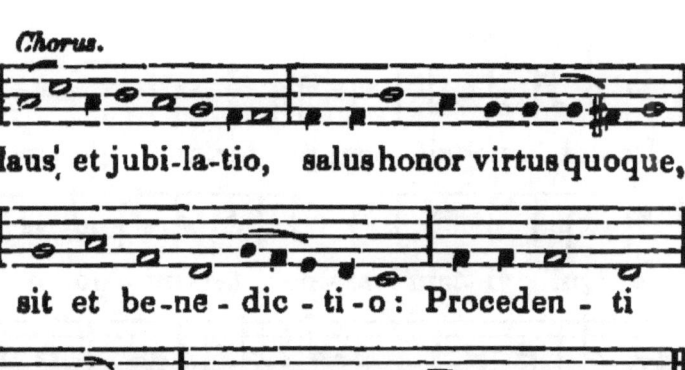

71—O SALUTARIS.

Do-mi - no sit sem-pi - ter-na glo - ri -a, Qui vi -tam si - ne ter-mi - no no- -bis do-net in pa - tri - a. A - men.

72—TE DEUM.

Te Deum lau-da - mus: Te Dominum

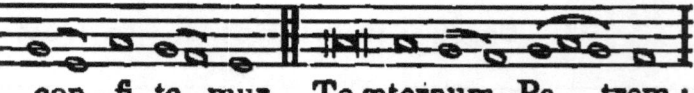
con - fi - te - mur. Te æternum Pa - trem:

omnis terra ve - ne-ra - tur. Tibi òm-nes

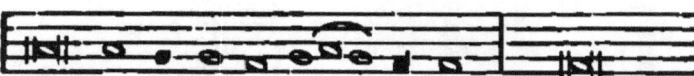
an - ge-li: tibi cœli et universæ potestates.

Tibi Cherubim et Se - raphim: incessabili

Et laudamus nomen tu-um in sæculum: et in sæculum sæculi. Dignare Domine die is-to: sine peccato nos cus-to-di-re. Miserere nos-tri Do-mine: mise-re-re nos-tri. Fiat misericordia tua Do-mi-ne su-per nos; quemadmodum spe-ra-vimus in Te. In Te Domine spera-vi: non confundar in-æternum.

73—AVE MARIS STELLA.

A-ve Ma-ris stel-la De-i Mater Al-ma, at-que semper Vir-

-go Felix cœli porta.

Monstra te esse Matrem su-

-mat per te preces: Qui pro nobis na-

- - -tus tulit se es tuus.

74—DE PROFUNDIS.

De profundis clamavi ad te Domine:

Domine exaudi vocem meam. &c.

75—MISERERE.

Miserere me-î Deus, secundum magnam

misericordiam tuam Et secundum multitudi-

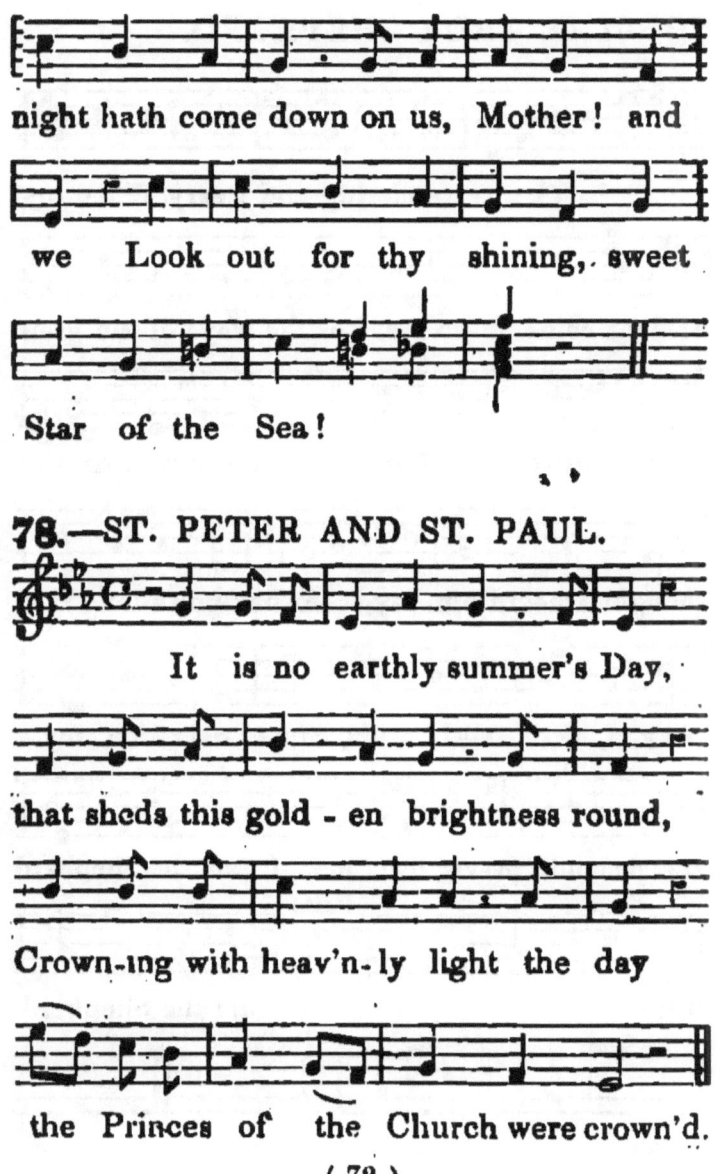

night hath come down on us, Mother! and we Look out for thy shining, sweet Star of the Sea!

78.—ST. PETER AND ST. PAUL.

It is no earthly summer's Day, that sheds this gold-en brightness round, Crown-ing with heav'n-ly light the day the Princes of the Church were crown'd.

79.—THE TRUE SHEPHERD.

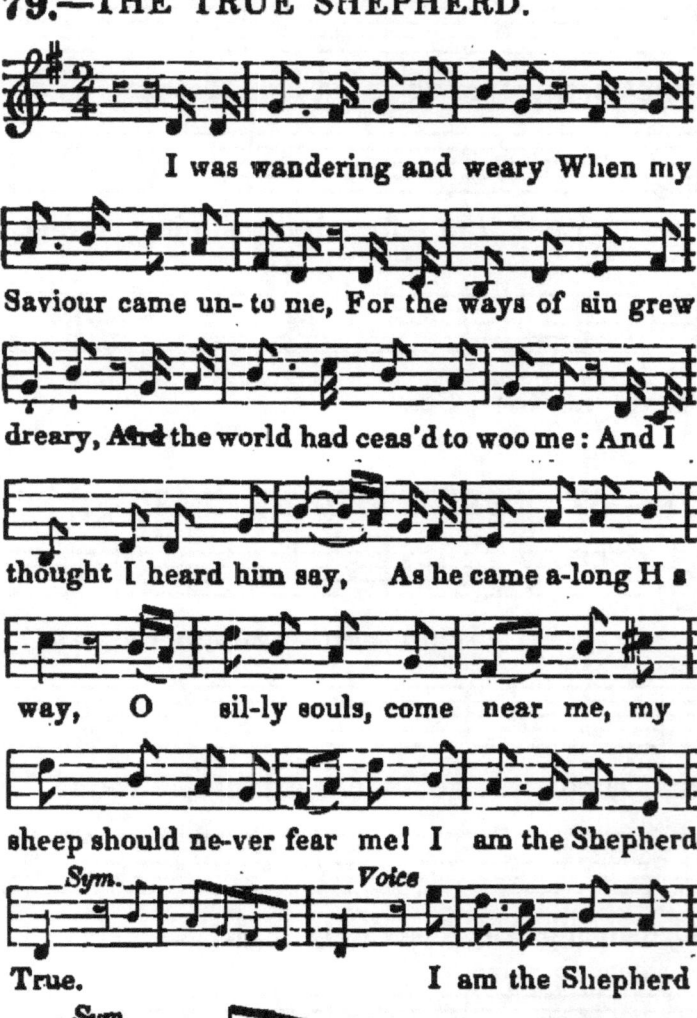

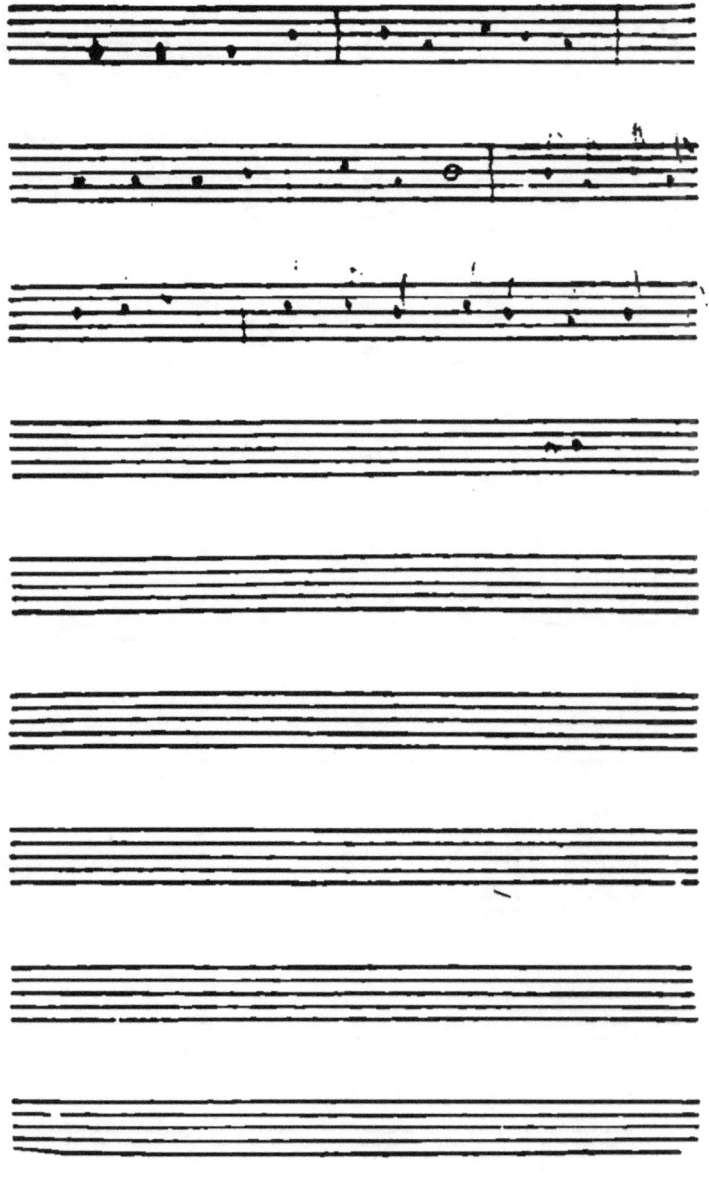

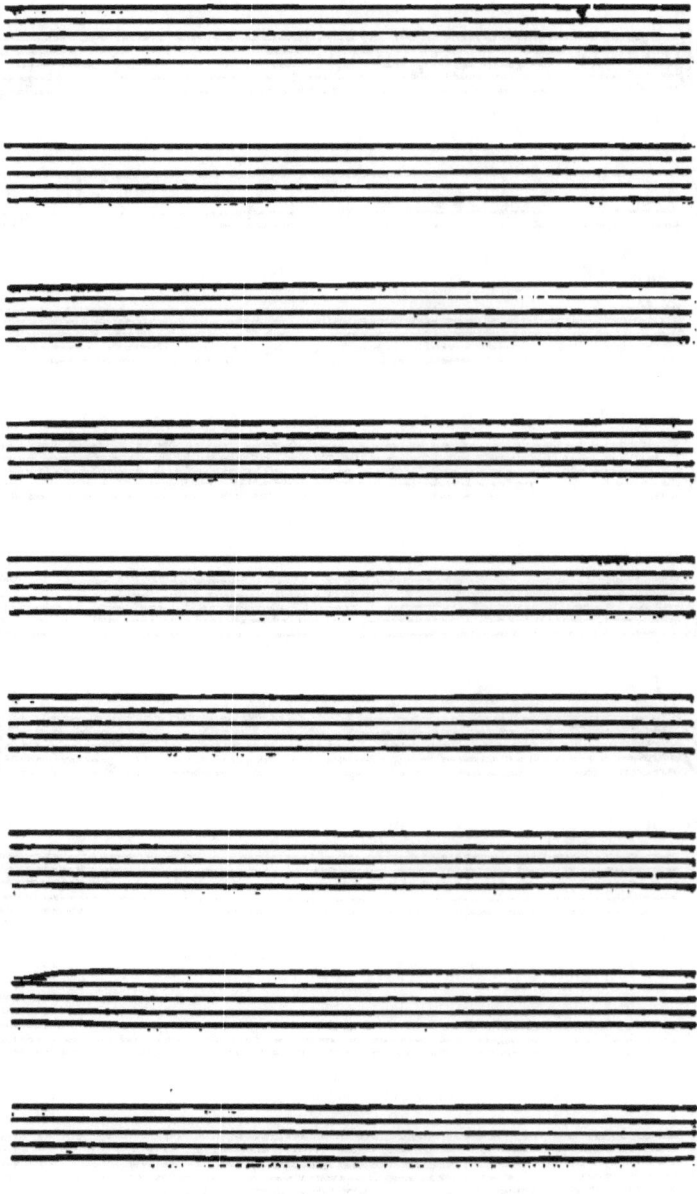

PUBLICATIONS OF THE ORATORY.

HYMNS OF THE ORATORY. New and enlarged edition. Price 6*d*.

MUSIC FOR DITTO. Price 1*s*.

⁎ The above may also be had together. Cloth, 2*s*.

DEVOTIONS TO THE INFANT JESUS. For Advent and other times. Price 2*d*.

NOVENA OF THE IMMACULATE CONCEPTION, AND OCTAVE FOR THE SOULS IN PURGATORY. Price 1*d*.

CHAPLET OF THE LOVE OF GOD. With the Indulgences. Price ½*d*.

ST. MARY MAGDALENE OF PAZZI'S WONDERFUL PRAYER FOR THE CONVERSION OF SINNERS. Price ½*d*.

THE PRAYER-BOOK OF THE ORATORY. Price 3*d*.

WAY OF THE CROSS; or, Book of the Stations. Price 2*d*.

Publications of the Oratory.

THE PASSION OF JESUS AND THE WOES OF MARY: the Lent-Book of the Oratory. Price 1½d.

JESUS RISEN: the Easter Book of the Oratory. Price 1d.

A MANUAL OF CONFESSION AND COMMUNION, for those who frequent the Oratory. Price 3d. each. Cloth, 6d.

BOOK OF THE CONFRATERNITY OF THE PRECIOUS BLOOD. Price 1d.

HOW TO BE A SAINT: A Rule of Life for those who frequent the Oratory. Price 2d.

THE WHITSUNTIDE BOOK OF THE ORATORY: Devotions to the Holy Ghost and Most Holy Trinity. Price 2d.

BOOK OF THE SACRED HEART. Price 2d.

SPIRIT AND GENIUS OF ST. PHILIP: a Triduo. Price 2s.

THE SCHOOL OF ST. PHILIP NERI. Edited by FATHER FABER. Price 5s.

Messrs. BURNS & LAMBERT, 17 PORTMAN STREET, PORTMAN SQUARE.

www.ingramcontent.com/pod-product-compliance
Lightning Source LLC
Chambersburg PA
CBHW020900230426
43666CB00008B/1259